Healing
Health Care

This book is available in e-book formats at: mnhealthplan.org

Individual printed copies are available from booksellers as well as directly from the publisher. Enclose $15 per book plus $10 shipping per order to Birch Grove Publishing, PO Box 131327, Roseville, MN 55113. For inquiries send email to publisher@birchgrovepublishing.com

EPUB ISBN:	978-1-945148-02-6
MOBI ISBN:	978-1-945148-03-3
PDF ISBN:	978-1-945148-04-0
PRINT ISBN:	978-1-945148-01-9

A MINNESOTA HEALTH PLAN

Healing Health Care

The Case for a Commonsense Universal Health System

John Marty

Birch Grove Publishing

Contents

Preface

In my travels throughout Minnesota and the country, I have seen firsthand the pain that our health care system has caused:

- The administrative nightmare for families trying to sort through medical bills and insurance paperwork.

- The financial burden that stresses all businesses and households, bankrupting those who had the misfortune to need care that destroyed their finances as much as their health.

- The moral toll that kills innocent people who gambled with their health because the financial cost was more than they could bear.

During my 30 years in the Minnesota Senate, I have seen firsthand the failure of our political system to seriously address health policy. In the United States, we squander outstanding health care resources—providers, clinics and hospitals, medical research and technology—on a broken system that makes it difficult and expensive for many people to get the care they need.

Why would any society make it *difficult* for its people to access health care?

I wrote this book because I am tired of waiting while our political process spends billions of dollars but merely tinkers at the edges of our health care problems.

- First we take a few steps back and look at the mess we have. By doing so, we identify the problems, develop principles for a healthy health care system, and map out a logical plan based on those principles.

- Then we work through our civic process and political system, make the case for our proposal, and then work to implement that plan.

This proposed Minnesota Health Plan and the principles that underlie it are nothing more than what any caring society would desire in order to ensure good health care for all of its people.

Acknowledgments

In developing the Minnesota Health Plan, I have been blessed with many excellent teachers, colleagues, and collaborators. They have inspired and encouraged me, and helped pull together the research and documentation to develop both the Minnesota Health Plan and this book.

Many people have contributed, but I especially want to acknowledge the tireless work, thoughtful advice, constant pushback, and challenging ideas which helped refine this proposal and this book from Barb Jacobs, Hannah Pallmeyer, Joel Clemmer, Kip Sullivan, Ellen Lafans, Dave Dvorak, Rebecca Bormann, Val Swenson, Inge DeBecker, Laurel Gamm, Taina Maki, Laura Kentnesse, Eileen Weber, Bryan Polkey, Nicole Dailey, Rose Roach, and Paul Nockleby. I am grateful to them and to all who have spoken and continue to speak out for universal health care.

Finally, I could not have written this without the incredible love and support of my family, Connie, Elsa, and Micah, who have given me the space to work for real reform, while providing great advice, ideas, and editorial assistance. I dedicate this book to them.

1. A Call to Action

If twenty-first century progressives had been leading the nineteenth century abolition movement, we would still have slavery, but we would have limited slavery to a 40-hour work week, and we would be congratulating each other on the progress we had made.

In earlier eras of U.S. history, progressives believed they could fight injustice and move society forward, and they did so—in the abolition movement, in women's suffrage, in social security for the elderly. Today, however, many progressive-minded people seem to have lost faith in our ability to bring about significant change. Many believe we must be content simply to tinker with problems.

Despite the reality that men were the only ones who held office and were the only ones who could vote, suffragettes fought and won the seemingly impossible goal of gaining the right to vote. In the 1960s, civil rights activists believed they could get rid of segregation laws and get equal rights under the law. When told they were expecting change to occur too rapidly, Martin Luther King wrote a book explaining, *"Why We Can't Wait."*

Today, however, regardless of the speed of other changes in society, many progressive-minded people have lost hope. Many politicians these days would more likely write a book titled, *"Why We Need to be Pragmatic and Accept Token Change."*

This timidity might be partially explained by decades of defeat at the hands of powerful financial interests and politicians beholden to those interests. But the result has been that many politicians who espouse progressive change have retreated from a "Politics of Principle" to a supposed "Politics of Pragmatism."

Under this misguided pragmatism, public officials and

political strategists calculate what they believe is politically acceptable, and *then* determine what they will stand for. Back in 2009, it was this "pragmatism" that led President Obama to push for health *insurance* for more instead of health *care* for all.

President Obama fought for and passed a "universal" health care system that isn't universal. The design of the Affordable Care Act was focused more on a sense of pragmatism than on real public health.

Unfortunately, that retreat from principle to pragmatism is not only lacking in courage, it hasn't been successful in moving us forward. In other words, it hasn't been very pragmatic. While the number of people who are insured has grown, there are large numbers of Americans (including Minnesotans) who are still unable to access the care they need, many of whom already have health insurance coverage.

After decades of calling for universal health care, which exists in virtually all other industrialized nations, it is time to stop pushing these "pragmatic" solutions that are not pragmatic. They have failed to even come close to delivering on a goal that already commands strong popular support.

Refusing to fight for something because it is "not politically realistic" becomes a self-fulfilling prophecy.

Here I speak from personal experience. There have been many times during my tenure in the Minnesota State Senate where I proposed legislation that pundits considered "lost causes"—proposals with no chance of passing.

The pundits were wrong. Success might not occur overnight, but it does happen, even in seemingly "hopeless" cases.

An excellent example comes from 2008, when I introduced legislation proposing marriage equality for LGBT couples. At the time, even the strongest advocates considered the idea to be decades away. I stated that I thought Minnesota could pass the legislation in about five years, not as a prediction, but to show it was a viable proposal.

Five years later, in August 2013, the month that Minnesota's marriage equality law took effect, an acquaintance approached me saying he wanted to apologize. I asked why. He responded, "Back in 2008, you introduced marriage equality legislation and said you thought it could pass in five years. I told all of my friends that you were crazy. I knew it would never happen in my lifetime."

The efforts of thousands of people who refused to accept inequality, made the "impossible" happen. And, they made it happen far faster than most people could imagine. "Politically unrealistic" proposals are not necessarily politically unrealistic unless we give up without trying.

If we begin with a logically designed health care system, one that addresses the flaws in our system, it might not be easy to pass, but we can do it.

A Rare Opportunity for Minnesota

Under the Affordable Care Act Section 1332, Minnesota has the opportunity to implement a new, innovative system to deliver health care. States can apply for an "innovation waiver" (waiving federal requirements of the ACA) starting in 2017. These waivers can be obtained as long as a state's plan provides at least as comprehensive of benefits, to at least as many people, and is at least as affordable as the Affordable Care Act. This is a rare, once-in-a-generation opportunity to restructure our health care system in a logical manner. We could accomplish this with the proposed Minnesota Health Plan described in this book and introduced at the Minnesota state capitol.

In earlier eras of U.S. history, progressive-minded people believed they could fight injustice and move society forward, and they did so. Today, we can too. It's time to have the courage of our convictions and push for a solution that is truly universal, such as the Minnesota Health Plan.

2. Healing Our Health Care System

A. Our Health Care Crisis

The United States has some of the best medical care available in the world. We have some of the best doctors, nurses, and other medical providers. We have some of the best hospitals and clinics, some of the best medical researchers and facilities, some of the best medical technology inventors and manufacturers. Minnesotans see our state as a leader in the nation, with some of the best of the best.

Despite all of these excellent medical resources our results are less than ideal because there are huge barriers to accessing that care. The result is less healthy people. Comparing our outcomes to other industrialized nations, the U.S. does not do very well in some basic health indicators. For instance, we have one of the worst infant mortality rates in the industrialized world[1] and our life expectancy is much lower than many other nations.[2]

Expensive

One of the main reasons many people do not have good access to health care is cost. Despite passage of the Affordable Care Act, almost a third of American adults struggle to pay for medical care, with many going deep into debt over it.[3] Even people who have health insurance do not always get the care they need because treatments

---

1   Marian F. MacDorman, et al., "International Comparisons of Infant Mortality and Related Factors: United States and Europe, 2010," *National Vital Statistics Report*, 63:5 (September 24, 2014), http://www.cdc.gov/nchs/data/nvsr/nvsr63/nvsr63_05.pdf.

2   Organization for Economic Co-operation and Development (OECD), "Life Expectancy at Birth," https://data.oecd.org/healthstat/life-expectancy-at-birth.htm#indicator-chart.

3   Karen Pollitz, et al., "Medical Debt Among People With Health Insurance," Kaiser Family Foundation, January 7, 2014, http://kff.org/private-insurance/report/medical-debt-among-people-with-health-insurance.

are not covered, or because they face high deductibles, co-pays, and other out-of-pocket costs.

We spend much more on health care than any other nation—about twice as much as other industrialized nations.[4] In 2012, people in the U.S. paid an average of $8,745 per person. Germany was about half that at $4,811 per person; Canada was $4,602; France was $4,288; and Japan was $3,649. In fact, the second most expensive country in the world was Norway at $6,140—fully $2,600 per person less than the US pays![5]

In addition to total cost, the way we decide who is responsible for those costs is highly inequitable. Unlike other industrialized countries, the amount an American has to pay for premiums, co-pays, and other out-of-pocket expenses for health care is usually not determined by that person's income.[6]

Because many people with serious and chronic health conditions have low incomes, health care is often least affordable to those who need it most. Conversely, many Minnesotans who are best able to afford health care have the best employer-paid coverage, with the lowest deductibles and co-pays.

Unfortunately, even with the passing of the Affordable Care Act, out-of-pocket expenses continue to rise for

---

4 Kaiser Family Foundation, "Snapshots: Health Care Spending in the United States & Selected OECD Countries," April 12, 2011, http://kff.org/health-costs/issue-brief/snapshots-health-care-spending-in-the-united-states-selected-oecd-countries.

5 OECD, "Total Expenditure on Health Per capita," June 30, 2014, http://www.oecd-ilibrary.org/social-issues-migration-health/total-expenditure-on-health-per-capita_20758480-table2.

6 Some state and federal health care programs such as Medicaid, MinnesotaCare, and the Affordable Care Act premium subsidies, are tied to income and designed to alleviate affordability problems. However, these programs are not always inadequate to the task of making health care affordable to people in the programs. Also, many others who cannot afford care do not qualify for them.

many who cannot afford it. To make sure they have some insurance coverage, they purchase policies with high deductibles and co-pays. "Silver" insurance plans on the MNsure exchange leave the average patient on the hook for 30% of their medical expenses in a given year. "Bronze" plans leave patients responsible for 40%.[7] Because health spending in the United States is currently over $9,500 per person,[8] the average person with a silver or bronze plan may end up paying a few thousand dollars in medical expenses *above* their insurance premiums.

This creates a Catch 22, where those who can only afford a cheaper insurance product are stuck with out-of-pocket expenses they cannot afford. When they become sick they don't go to the doctor because of cost, or if they do go, they struggle to pay the bill.

While the ACA provides subsidies for some, insurance purchased on the exchange is still unaffordable to many people because of out-of-pocket expenses.[9] Funding for our current health system is inconsistent and illogical. Poor Minnesotans on Medicaid have good coverage, but others whose income is slightly higher get poor coverage.

The working poor often earn too much to qualify for Medicaid, and they are generally the people with the worst coverage. Many people do not have any dental coverage whatsoever, and one of every five adults with

---

7 HealthCare.Gov, "Understanding Marketplace Health Insurance Categories," https://www.healthcare.gov/choose-a-plan/plans-categories/.
8 Health care spending in the United States was $9523 per person in 2014 and projected to grow by 4.9% per year. See Centers for Medicare and Medicaid Services (CMS), "NHE Fact Sheet," https://www.cms.gov/Research-Statistics-Data-and-Systems/Statistics-Trends-and-Reports/NationalHealthExpendData/NHE-Fact-Sheet.html.
9 Michael Ollove, "Affording the Affordable Care Act," *Pew Charitable Trusts*, January 14, 2014, http://www.pewtrusts.org/en/research-and-analysis/blogs/stateline/2014/01/14/affording-the-affordable-care-act.

health insurance reports unmet dental needs because of affordability.[10]

Minnesota does better than other states in providing health insurance coverage: almost 96% of Minnesotans are covered.[11] However, even now that the Affordable Care Act (ACA) has been fully implemented, there are over 200,000 Minnesotans without any health insurance.[12]

There are also at least a million more Minnesotans who have insurance, but still cannot afford the care they need due to co-payments, deductibles, and care not covered by their insurance.[13] The Minnesota Health Plan would eliminate the problem of being uninsured or underinsured. It would also address other barriers to care. In addition to insurance coverage, provider shortages and limited provider networks covered by an insurance plan are also barriers to care.

In January 2016, members of a recent state health care reform task force[14] heard from an advocate for farmers[15]

---

10 Adele Shartzer and Genevieve M. Kenney, "QuickTake: The Forgotten Health Care Need: Gaps in Dental Care for Insured Adults Remain under ACA," *Health Reform Monitoring Survey*, Sept. 24, 2015, Fig. 2, http://hrms.urban.org/quicktakes/Gaps-in-Dental-Care-for-Insured-Adults-Remain-under-ACA.html.
11 Minnesota Department of Health, "Health Insurance Coverage in Minnesota: Results from the 2015 Minnesota Health Access Survey," February 29, 2016, http://www.health.state.mn.us/divs/hpsc/hep/publications/coverage/healthinscovmnhas2015brief.pdf.
12 Ibid. 234,000 Minnesotans lack coverage.
13 That is a conservative estimate. According to the Commonwealth Fund, in 2012, 43% of Americans did not get the care they needed because of cost. With almost 5.5 million Minnesotans, that would leave over 2 million people not getting needed care if Minnesota's rate was as bad as the national rate. Sara R. Collins, Ruth Robertson, Tracy Garber, and Michelle M. Doty, "Insuring the Future: Current Trends in Health Coverage and the Effects of Implementing the Affordable Care Act," *The Commonwealth Fund*, April 2013, Exhibit ES-3, http://www.commonwealthfund.org/~/media/files/publications/fund-report/2013/apr/1681_collins_insuring_future_biennial_survey_2012_final.pdf.
14 2015 Task Force on Health Care Financing.
15 A farm advocate from the Land Stewardship Project.

about a Minnesotan living just north of the Iowa border who had health insurance but needed oral surgery. The woman searched across southern Minnesota and could only find one oral surgeon who would accept her medical assistance insurance plan. Unfortunately, he had a waiting list of 150 people. She called a Delta Dental "hotline" that guarantees they will find dental care. The next closest dental providers they could find were in St. Paul and Richfield—at least two hours away. Even people with coverage may struggle to find a doctor who will accept their insurance and treat them.

Inefficient and Complex

Another barrier to care is the cumbersome insurance bureaucracy. The farm advocate referenced above also told task force members about a couple from west central Minnesota who received a letter notifying them that their coverage was being dropped at the end of the month. The letter was sent because the re-enrollment forms they had submitted were overlooked. The couple had done nothing wrong, but still expended much time, energy and emotional distress getting their coverage reinstated. Complicated eligibility and application rules make insurance programs hard to administer and prone to mistakes.

State and federal government programs each have their own eligibility requirements, and most require selection of an insurance company. Each insurance company has numerous different products to choose from, each with their own rules and restrictions related to provider networks, benefit sets, and levels of cost sharing. For 2016, the MNsure exchange had 100 different plans just for the individual and family market.[16]

---

16 MNsure, "Health Care Coverage and Plan Rates for 2016: A Snapshot of 2016 Premiums and Tax Credits," p.2, https://www.mnsure.org/images/2016-MNsure-healthcare-coverage-plan-rates.pdf

Each of these entities—the consumer, the government, and the insurance companies—all need to share enrollment information with each other, but still maintain confidentiality. It is a highly complex undertaking just to enroll people.

Contrast the expense and difficulties faced by **MNsure** to the enrollment of seniors in **Medicare** five decades ago. Using file cabinets and index cards—they had no computer technology—Medicare was able to enroll virtually all 19 million American seniors in a matter of months[17] because the system was simple. They didn't have to deal with multiple insurers with multiple plans offering multiple benefit sets and differing provider networks; instead, Medicare enrollees had one high quality plan that covered everyone over age 65.

The difference in costs is evidence of the simplicity. It cost the federal government $120 million in overhead costs for Medicare in the first year to enroll seniors and administer the claims.[18] Inflation adjusted, that is $867 million in 2013. In contrast, the federal government spent at least $6 billion to set up the state and federal health exchanges under the ACA and complete the first year of enrollment.[19]

Even after a couple of years, by 2015 the total enrollment in the exchanges was less than 12 million people nationwide.[20] This comparison shows that after two years

17   David Himmelstein and Steffie Woolhandler, "Medicare's Rollout vs. Obamacare's Glitches Brew," *Health Affairs*, January 2, 2014, http://healthaffairs.org/blog/2014/01/02/medicares-rollout-vs-obamacares-glitches-brew.

18   Ibid.

19   Ibid.

20   11.7 million people were enrolled in health coverage through the exchanges by February 2015. HHS news release, March 10, 2015, http://www.hhs.gov/about/news/2015/03/10/nationwide-nearly-11-point-7-million-consumers-are-enrolled-in-2015-health-insurance-marketplace-coverage.html.

the exchanges enrolled less than 2/3 as many people as Medicare did in its first year, yet it cost seven times as much in administrative costs.

Per enrollee, it cost at least ten times as much to enroll people in the ACA exchanges as it cost to enroll people in Medicare! The differential in costs is even more stunning when accounting for the fact that those Medicare costs for the first year of operation *included* administration of all the medical bills, while the exchanges do not handle any of the claims processing, just enrollment. "So billions more in overhead costs will show up on the books of the private insurers and state Medicaid programs that will actually process medical claims," says Dr. David Himmelstein.[21]

Disjointed

To deal with our high health care costs and poor outcomes, our political system continually seeks reforms that will decrease costs and improve coverage. In Minnesota, there have been more than a dozen state task forces and commissions created by legislators and governors over the past few decades[22] to reform the health care system. Unfortunately, despite all of their hard work, we are not close to ending this health care crisis.

One of the difficulties in solving our various health care problems has been the lack of a unified entity that is

---

21 David Himmelstein and Steffie Woolhandler, "Medicare's Rollout vs. Obamacare's Glitches Brew," *Health Affairs*, January 2, 2014, http://healthaffairs.org/blog/2014/01/02/medicares-rollout-vs-obamacares-glitches-brew.

22 Task Force on Health Care Financing (2015), Health Care Reform Task Force (2011), Health Insurance Exchange Advisory Task Force (2011), Health Care Reform Task Force (2010), Health Care Reform Review Council (2008-10), Health Care Transformation Task Force (2007-08), Legislative Commission on Health Care Access (2007), Governor Pawlenty's Citizens Forum on Health Care Costs (2003), Health Care Commission (HealthRight) (1992-97), Legislative Commission on Health Care Access (1992), Health Care Access Commission (1989-91), Governor Quie's Task Force on Health Care (1981), Governor Perpich's Task Force on Insurance and Health (1978-79).

actually responsible for making sure Minnesotans receive health care when and where they need it. This applies not only to whether individuals have health coverage, but all aspects of the system such as ensuring an appropriate number of health care providers and implementing public health initiatives.

While some health systems and health plans currently have some good public health initiatives in place, those efforts are understandably aimed at their own patients or members. None of the health plans are likely to direct public health resources at the broader public or specific demographic segments of it, because most people are not enrolled in their plan. As a result, there is far less investment in public health than there would be under a universal health care system and far less ability to target public health initiatives wisely. For example, some research suggests our infant mortality rates would improve with universal postnatal care, such as having a home visit from a nurse as they do in some European countries.[23]

All of the gaps in our system cause problems. Some of the problems make the system too costly, some prevent us from improving health, and some result in people failing to get the medical care that they need. Unfortunately, we have become accustomed to this broken system.

It is not acceptable, and will never be acceptable, for people to have gaps in their health coverage, or to lose that coverage entirely. Fixing these problems will require fundamental changes in our health care system. We need a new model.

---

23   Alice Chen, Emily Oster, and Heidi Williams, "Why Is Infant Mortality Higher in the US Than in Europe?" *National Bureau of Economic Research Working Paper Series,* Working Paper 20525, http://www.nber.org/papers/w20525.pdf.

B. Health Care Should Be Covered Like Police and Fire

Nobody in Minnesota goes without police and fire protection—nobody has to apply for new "police and fire coverage" each year, nobody has to worry that they may no longer be qualified, nobody has to worry about a $3,000 deductible before the fire department will come. Nobody has to worry that the local sheriff won't accept their "police insurance" plan. And nobody gets a letter informing them that their police or fire coverage is being terminated at the end of the month, for any reason.

A civilized, humane society that takes care of its people with universal police and fire coverage needs to do the same with health and dental care.

C. Designing a Solution

Before starting out on a trip it is important to know where you are going: focus on your goals and where you are headed.

The same is true for designing a health care system. Instead of simply trying to reduce costs or cover more people by tinkering within the current system, we should begin by laying out the requirements that we expect the system to meet. Only after spelling out the parameters is it time to design and implement a system to meet the goals.

Unfortunately, the American political system has never taken the time to spell out goals and design a health care system to meet them. Consequently, discussions about health care reform in Washington and St. Paul get wrapped up in ideology and efforts to score political points.

The debate—pro and con—over the Affordable Care Act is a case in point. People put so much energy into the politics and the political strategy that they forgot what they were hoping to accomplish.

The result is a hodgepodge of policy that doesn't make a lot of sense and has significant holes. The extent of dysfunction in our system is so great that one business executive quipped, "If you tried to design a health care system that *didn't* work, you couldn't have done a better job [than what we have now.]"[24]

D. Principles for Health Care

It is time that we step back, map out our direction, and spell out the principles that we want our health care system to meet. Here are ten principles that need to be followed if a health care system is to serve the public well. The health care system must:

- ensure all people are covered;
- cover all types of care, including dental, vision and hearing, mental health, chemical dependency treatment, prescription drugs, medical equipment and supplies, long-term care, and home care;
- allow patients to choose their providers;
- reduce costs by cutting administrative bureaucracy, not by restricting or denying care;
- set premiums based on ability to pay;
- focus on preventive care and early intervention to improve health;
- ensure there are enough health care providers to guarantee timely access to care;
- continue Minnesota's leadership in medical education, research, and technology;
- provide adequate and timely payments to providers; and
- use a simple funding and payment system.

---

24 Tom Forsythe, Vice President, General Mills, 2007.

All of these principles are important; all need to be met.

There may be a variety of ways in which Minnesota could meet these principles. One proposal to do so is called the **Minnesota Health Plan (MHP)**.[25] The MHP is *designed* to meet all of these principles, and it would be *governed* by them as well. The principles would be legally binding on the board of the MHP,[26] setting it apart from other health systems in its focus on public health and well-being instead of profit or politics.

---

25 2015-16 legislation: Senate File 2060 (Marty) /House File 2209 (Laine). The full text of the bill is available online: http://tinyurl.com/MHP-2016-bill. The legislation will have new bill numbers when reintroduced in 2017.
26 tinyurl.com/MHP-2016-bill, p. 1.13, 14.23.

3. The Minnesota Health Plan

A Brief Introduction

The Minnesota Health Plan (also referred to as "MHP" or "the plan") is a proposed comprehensive health care system for Minnesota. While it is what is often called a "single-payer" health plan, the MHP is much more than just a method of paying for health care. It is an entire health care system designed to improve patient access and experience, improve health outcomes, and increase support for health care providers.

The MHP would be a single statewide plan that covers all Minnesotans for all their medical needs.[27] Under the MHP, patients would be able to see the medical providers of their choice, and their coverage would not end if they lose their job or switch to a new employer. Dental care, prescription drugs, optometry, mental health services, chemical dependency treatment, and medical equipment and supplies would all be covered, as well as home care services and nursing home care. Application forms would be short and simple, and there would be no confusion over whether a treatment is covered and no worrying about how to afford the drugs you need.

People could use the same doctors and medical professionals as they do now. They could also use the same hospitals and clinics, which would remain under their existing ownership, whether public or private. Payments to health care providers would be made by the MHP instead of from multiple insurance companies, reducing administrative bureaucracy and saving money. The MHP would restore medical decision-making to the doctor and patient, eliminating insurance company interference. Additionally, the MHP would be responsible

---

27 Ibid., p. 2.30, 4.27.

for ensuring health provider adequacy around the state, addressing access problems beyond cost.

The Minnesota Health Plan would be prohibited from restricting, delaying, or denying care or reducing quality to save money. Instead, the MHP would save money through elimination of the insurance bureaucracy, negotiation of prices, simplification of billing, payment, and administrative systems, and improved health outcomes.

The MHP would facilitate ongoing improvements in health care quality and delivery, and would give medical providers the opportunity to negotiate a fair, rational compensation system while freeing them from burdensome administrative paperwork.

In recognition of the significant changes in the workforce that would take place under the MHP, the bill includes retraining and other dislocated worker benefits for administrative workers displaced in the transition to the new health plan.

The plan would be funded by all Minnesotans, based on their ability to pay, and would cover all health care costs, replacing all premiums currently paid as well as all co-payments, deductibles, and all payments for care of the uninsured or under-insured.

Finally, the MHP will save families, businesses, and providers time, money, and emotional stress over finding coverage and paying for care.

The MHP would be governed by a democratically selected board, which would be legally bound to a set of principles that ensure that the public interest is served.

Although the Minnesota Health Plan is not cheap, it is significantly less expensive than our current system and it would provide a full range of health care services to everyone, greatly improving the health of the population.

The Minnesota Health Plan would be created through legislation (in 2016, it was Senate File 2060/House File 2209).[28] The following pages describe and explain components of the MHP.

A. Everyone is Covered

The Minnesota Health Plan covers all Minnesota residents. When Minnesotans travel out of state, the coverage would travel with them, reimbursing the providers who treat them.[29]

Nonresidents receiving medical services in Minnesota would be billed for those services, just as they are currently.[30] The MHP would offer coverage to nonresidents who are employed in Minnesota (they would pay premiums just as Minnesotans do).[31]

For people moving from other states to get care in Minnesota because they cannot afford the care they need in their home state, the MHP board would seek federal authority to bill those states for their health care costs.[32]It is not Minnesota's responsibility to fill in the gaps in other states' coverage for their residents. If people move here because their home states fail to provide such coverage, Minnesota should be able to bill those states for the services provided, unless those states establish reciprocal agreements to provide similar coverage to Minnesotans moving to them.[33]

Retirees living in Minnesota would have all of their Medicare benefits (and retiree health benefits from an employer if they have them), *plus* they would have all other

---

28 Ibid.
29 Ibid., p. 3.3.
30 Ibid., p. 3.11.
31 Ibid., p. 3.15.
32 Ibid., p. 16.11.
33 Ibid., p. 16.13.

MHP benefits. If retirees move out of state, they would retain their Medicare and other retiree health benefits.[34]

Quick and Easy Enrollment

Similar to the start of Medicare back in 1966,[35] the Minnesota Health Plan would be simple to enroll in, with a straightforward one or two-page enrollment form.[36] It would be simple because all Minnesotans are eligible regardless of income, employment status, age, location or number of family members, and there is no need to choose a bronze, silver, gold, or platinum plan. The MHP avoids the bureaucratic complexity of our current system. It would be as quick and easy to enroll one's family in the MHP as it is to enroll one's child in the local elementary school.

It is not an overstatement to say that the MHP would eliminate the (often annual) hassle faced by most families and businesses in selecting the appropriate plan to meet their needs. It would eliminate the hassle of determining whether a clinic or provider is "in network." It would eliminate the hassle of guessing how much care one will need in the coming year for pre-tax medical expense accounts. It would also eliminate the hassle of guessing

---

34 Ibid., p. 3.20.
35 "Signing up most of the elderly for Medicare was simple; they were already known to Social Security Administration, which handled enrollment. To find the rest, the feds sent out mailings to seniors, held local meetings, and asked postal workers, forest rangers and agricultural representatives to help contact people in remote areas. The Office for Economic Opportunity spent $14.5 million to hire 5,000 low income seniors who went door-to-door in their neighborhoods. Despite predictions of chaos, and worries that the newly-insured seniors would flood the health care system, there were few bottlenecks. Hospitals continued to operate smoothly and no waiting lists materialized. The only real "glitch" was that many hospitals in the Deep South initially refused to integrate their facilities..." David Himmelstein and Steffie Woolhandler, "Medicare's Rollout vs. Obamacare's Glitches Brew," Health Affairs, January 2, 2014, http://healthaffairs.org/blog/2014/01/02/medicares-rollout-vs-obamacares-glitches-brew.
36 tinyurl.com/MHP-2016-bill, p. 3.1.

whether additional insurance is needed for things not usually covered by standard health insurance plans, like dental care or nursing home care. Employers would not need to assign staff to explain to employees what the changes in benefits and providers are each year. It would be simple and hassle-free.

Simplicity matters, as is evident from the troubled roll-out of the MNsure health insurance exchange. While MNsure has helped many Minnesotans get health insurance coverage, the complexity of the endeavor continues to stymie even top programming experts brought in by the state to fix its glitches.

B. Comprehensive Benefits

Under the Minnesota Health Plan, medically appropriate care would be completely covered. Dental care would not be an "extra," nor would long term care. Prescription drugs would be covered without any "doughnut hole." Mental health would be treated as seriously as physical health.

The MHP would cover:[37]

- inpatient and outpatient care
- primary and specialized care
- emergency care and transportation
- diagnostic imaging and lab services
- medical equipment, supplies (such as insulin), and assistive technology (such as prosthetics, eyeglasses, and hearing aids)
- health care transportation for people with disabilities or low income
- immunizations and preventive care

---

37 Ibid., p. 4.27.

- health and wellness education
- hospice care
- nursing home care
- home health care
- mental health services
- substance abuse (chemical dependency) treatment
- dental care
- vision and hearing care
- prescription drugs–with no Medicare "doughnut hole"
- podiatric care
- chiropractic care
- acupuncture
- complementary and alternative medicine therapies shown to be safe and effective
- blood and blood products
- dialysis
- adult day care
- occupational and physical therapy and other rehabilitative and habilitative services
- ancillary health and social services for low income people currently covered by public health programs, including services currently available under Home and Community Based Services (HCBS) waivers, such as cognitive retraining for people with brain injuries and supported employment services
- case management and care coordination
- interpreter services, including sign language and Braille

Because the MHP provides comprehensive benefits, there are few exclusions. However, the MHP would not cover health services that provide no medical benefit. Also, purely cosmetic surgery would not be covered unless it is done to restore a congenital anomaly, to restore a part of the body that was altered by disease, injury, or surgery, or because it is medically necessary.[38]

For seniors, one could view the MN Health Plan as *Medicare Plus*—it would cover all Medicare benefits, *plus* dental care, *plus* long-term care, *plus* all of the benefits that currently require supplemental coverage, *plus* it would eliminate co-payments and deductibles. *Plus*, it would give those same benefits to people under age 65 as well.

Because the MHP provides comprehensive medical benefits and does not use co-pays and deductibles,[39] all Minnesotans will get the care they need, when they need it.

Primary Care Providers and Care Coordination

The MHP would encourage everyone to select a primary care provider who would coordinate their care and work with them on health improvement.[40] Care coordination can make sure immunizations are up to date and ensure that patients know where to turn for appropriate care. In addition, by keeping track of medical test results, there would be fewer repeat tests on patients by doctors who were unaware that the tests had already been performed.

Health Care Available by Phone 24/7

Many of the best health plans have a 24/7 nurse line available to their members. The MHP would offer this for everyone.[41] This enables people to find out whether their health care status merits a trip to the doctor. Making

---

38 Ibid., p. 6.10.
39 Ibid., p. 9.32.
40 Ibid., p. 6.24, 6.27.
41 Ibid., p. 19.1.

such help available not only reduces unnecessary trips to the emergency room, it also helps people to get the appropriate care, and can reduce anxiety among patients.

Patient Choice vs. Limited Networks

As has been evident during the political fighting over the Affordable Care Act, one of the biggest fears people have about health care reform is that they will lose their "freedom of choice."

Unfortunately, that entire debate about whether the ACA would take away "choice" presumed that the concern was over which insurance plan people could choose. It ignored the real question that people care about: "Will I be able to determine the type of care I receive and can I choose which doctors (and clinics, hospitals, dentists, and pharmacies) I use?"

Freedom to choose the health care providers a patient wants is guaranteed under the governing principles (and legal requirements) of the MHP.[42]

In contrast, under our current system, most people are limited to providers within their insurance network, or have to pay extra to see an "out-of-network" provider.

Determinations of who is "in" and "out" of network are becoming increasingly complex. In some cases, patients treated at in-network hospitals are served by out-of-network providers used by the hospital. Even some providers are confused about how to answer prospective patient questions about whether they are in- or out-of-network. As a result, there are cases where patients are hit with exorbitant bills from using an out-of-network provider that they mistakenly thought was in-network.[43]

---

42 Ibid., p. 1.22.
43 Karen Pollitz, "Surprise Medical Bills," *Kaiser Family Foundation*, March

The Minnesota Health Plan will eliminate the out-of-insurance network barrier to care by creating the biggest network yet: one that includes every medical provider.

One of the big benefits of giving patients the ability to choose their medical providers is improvement in continuity of care. Under our current insurance-based system some people are forced to change their personal doctors, clinics, and hospitals, not based on medical need, but because they switched jobs or their employer switched health plans. This replaces doctors who have their trust with new providers who do not know their medical history.

Doctors tell of the waste of time and money, as well as increased health risks, when they need to switch multiple medications for a patient because of a change in the covered drugs under the drug formulary due to a patient's change in health plans. Loss of continuity of care can put health at risk—it can lead to complications and increased hospitalizations—and it wastes the time and resources of both doctor and patient.

With patient choice, people will switch doctors if they want to, not because their employer switches health plans or their health plan changes its provider network.

Drug Formulary

Lastly, the problem of different drug formularies for different health plans will be eliminated. Doctors who receive new patients from other health plans can point to health risks as well as wasted time and money caused by the need to change prescriptions because drugs the patients were using are not on their new health plan's formulary. The MHP would cover all medically-necessary prescriptions.

17, 2016, http://kff.org/private-insurance/issue-brief/surprise-medical-bills/.

C. Financing

In American political discourse, the topic of financing universal health care draws comments about how "expensive" it will be from people who reference the additional costs without acknowledging the savings that will pay for those costs.

A number of studies have shown that when accounting for all sources of health care funding, there is already enough money in the system to cover everyone without increasing the total amount of money expended on health care, by cutting bureaucracy and other cost-saving measures.[44] The financing system for the MHP is designed to establish a fair manner of financing current health care costs, *not* to find a way to get more money into the system.

Of the estimated $50 billion in annual health care expenditures in Minnesota,[45] about half are paid by federal, state, and local governments and half are shared between individuals and businesses.[46] The MHP would likely allocate costs between government, businesses, and individuals in roughly the same proportion as now.

The MHP would use existing state and federal government funds—money already spent on programs such as Medicaid,

---

44 See "Economics of the Minnesota Health Plan" chapter.
45 $50.7 billion in 2016 projections from the Minnesota Department of Health, "Minnesota Health Care Spending and Projections, 2013," March 2016, Table 4, p. 26, http://www.health.state.mn.us/divs/hpsc/hep/publications/costs/healthspending2016.pdf.
46 Ibid. Of the $50.7 billion, public health spending is $23.7 billion, or 46.75% of the total, and private health spending is $27 billion or 53.25%. However, this public spending does NOT include public spending by the government on health insurance for public employees, nor does it include public "tax expenditures" in the form of tax exemptions for premiums paid by employers and employees, pre-tax, nor does it include the federal premium subsidies paid to many of the people who purchase health insurance through the MNsure insurance exchange, according to Stefan Gildemeister, MDH economist.

MinnesotaCare, Medicare, along with public employee health care coverage, federal tax breaks for employer-based coverage and MNsure subsidies—to pay for roughly half of the program. The other half would come from premiums from individuals and a payroll tax on businesses.

Individual Premiums

The Minnesota Health Plan would use a progressive payment system, with health care premiums based on ability to pay.[47] This solves the biggest problem related to health care access by making health care affordable to all. This progressive premium structure is necessary for fairness, for access, and for its positive impact on public health. Everybody pays, and everybody benefits.

Under the MHP, Minnesotans would have only one health care payment: their premiums. They would not be nickeled-and-dimed by co-pays, deductibles, payments for services not covered by their current insurance coverage or other out-of-pocket expenses. While some families may pay more, the vast majority of individuals and families would pay significantly less for health care under the MHP than they currently do under our insurance-based system.[48]

The Minnesota Health Plan premiums would likely be collected by the Department of Revenue, because the department already has a mechanism for collecting revenue, including revenue based on ability to pay (income).

---

47 tinyurl.com/MHP-2016-bill, p. 8.15.
48 According to the Lewin Group's study of a generic single payer plan in Minnesota, a Minnesota family with the median household income of $60,000/year would save an average of about $3,500/year. See John Sheils and Megan Cole, "Cost and Economic Impact Analysis of a Single-Payer Plan in Minnesota," *Growth & Justice*, March 27, 2012, p. 22, http://www. growthandjustice.org/images/uploads/LEWIN.Final_Report_FINAL_DRAFT.pdf.

Opponents might argue that the premiums paid for the Minnesota Health Plan should be called "taxes." However, unlike taxes, MHP premiums would not go to the state treasury; they would go directly to the Minnesota Health Plan.[49] They would only be used to pay for health care; they would not be used to balance the state budget or pay for anything else. Essentially, instead of paying premiums to an employer or a health insurance company, premiums would now be paid to the Minnesota Health Plan.

Business Payroll Tax

Under the MHP, businesses would pay a payroll tax in place of the premiums they pay for employee plans or penalties for not providing coverage under the Affordable Care Act. Some employers, such as ones who provide minimal health care benefits to their employees, may end up paying more, but most businesses would pay less than they currently pay.[50] All businesses would benefit from lifting the administrative burden of researching, choosing, and negotiating a health insurance plan every year or two. Businesses will also benefit from having healthier employees.

Government Funding

In addition to individual premiums and business payroll taxes, the MHP would use the federal and state funds spent on existing public health care programs.

---

49 tinyurl.com/MHP-2016-bill, p. 7.2, 7.5.

50 Employers offering health benefits to employees would see an average annual savings of about $1200 per employee, but employers who did not offer any health benefits would see an average increase of just over $2100 per employee, according to the Lewin Group's study of a generic single payer plan in Minnesota. See John Sheils and Megan Cole, "Cost and Economic Impact Analysis of a Single-Payer Plan in Minnesota," *Growth & Justice*, March 27, 2012, pp. 15-20, http://www.growthandjustice.org/images/uploads/LEWIN.Final_Report_FINAL_DRAFT.pdf.

The MHP would seek any waivers or agreements needed with the federal government to draw on federal funds currently allocated to Minnesota for health care. In exchange, the state would assume responsibility for health care services which had been covered by the federal government—including programs for seniors, veterans, federal employees, low income families, and people with disabilities.

If the MHP is unable to secure the federal funds, the federal government would continue paying for their programs as usual and the MHP would fill in gaps in coverage—paying co-pays, deductibles, and costs for care that federal programs do not cover.

Other Sources of Funding

There are also some smaller sources of funding that would help pay for health care under the MHP. If a person receives medical care that may be covered by some other source, such as a court judgment for damages for personal injury, the MHP would collect payment from that insurance or other collateral source.[51]

ERISA

Federal law prohibits states from regulating employee benefit plans under the Employee Retirement Income Security Act (ERISA).

The MHP is designed in a manner that does not interfere with employee benefit plans. The MHP leaves ERISA plans alone, simply establishing a universal health plan available to all Minnesotans. The taxing authority of the state finances the program for the public benefit and

---

51 These collateral sources of funds would come from situations such as an auto accident with a person insured in some other state, because Minnesota auto insurance would no longer need to cover medical expenses under the MHP. Obviously, this means that Minnesotans would save significantly in lower premiums for auto insurance, workers' compensation coverage, etc.

it does not require or prohibit employers from offering health care benefits to employees.

From an employee's perspective, the MHP would be an improvement—no employer provides better coverage and benefits than their workers would receive under the MHP, and co-pays and deductibles would end.

From a business perspective, most employers would be pleased to avoid the huge hassle and expense of providing health coverage for their employees, knowing those employees would have comprehensive coverage under the MHP. They would not need to continue their employee health plans, but the MHP legislation would not limit their ability to do so if they so choose.

D. Fair Treatment of Medical Providers

A recent Star Tribune story reported that "constant stress brought on by cost pressures and a changing system that many [physicians] feel is beyond their control" is leading to increasing physician burnout.[52] The additional paperwork from alternative payment systems is "almost universally disliked" by physicians and might also add stress,[53]

---

52 "Burnout has spiked with the adoption of computerized medical records… because many doctors believe the systems interfere with patient relationships. More cost-sharing for patients has stressed doctors, too, as physicians try to help patients get care with fewer out-of-pocket costs." See Christopher Snowbeck, "Minnesota Hospitals Ramp up Efforts to Battle Physician Burnout," *Star Tribune*, August 6, 2016, http://www.startribune.com/minnesota-hospitals-ramp-up-efforts-to-battle-physician-burnout/389385481/.

53 "Many respondents described increases [in stress and time pressure] associated with alternative payment models in the quantity and intensity of both clinical and nonclinical work for physicians… New nonclinical work for physicians was almost universally disliked, especially when there was no clear link to better patient care. For example, frustration was common when physicians believed they were being asked to spend more time on documentation solely to get credit for care they had provided already. Overall, increased stress on physicians might directly harm the quality of patient care and might also serve as a marker that physicians are concerned about the quality of care they are able to provide." See Mark

according to an AMA/RAND study. This is particularly troubling given our health care provider shortage.

Currently providers, especially small ones, are at the mercy of insurance companies and the government in seeking fair compensation. The reimbursement rate is dictated to them, without their input. Small, independent clinics have no negotiating clout against large insurance companies. Inadequate dental reimbursement rates under Medicaid are a good illustration of the problem.[54]

Several years ago, the Senate Health Committee heard testimony about patients having to travel over 60 miles each way to have dental work done because local dentists, including two clinics within a half mile of one patient's home, would not accept inadequate Medicaid compensation rates.[55] By reimbursing providers for all patients at a fair rate, on a timely basis, the MHP will prevent the problem of providers turning away Medicaid patients, which has forced many to travel long distances for care.

The Minnesota Health Plan gives providers the opportunity to negotiate a sustainable payment system.[56] With negotiated compensation, providers will have a voice in setting reimbursements so they are paid in a fair, logical manner—including for services that are currently not billable, but which contribute to healthier people. Additionally, the board would work to eliminate conflicts

---

W. Friedberg, et.al., "Effects of Health Care Payment Models on Physician Practice in the United States," *American Medical Association and the RAND Corporation*, March 19, 2015, p. 98, http://www.rand.org/content/dam/rand/pubs/research_reports/RR800/RR869/RAND_RR869.pdf.

54   Lorna Benson, "Report: Dentists Underpaid by State for Low-Income Patient Care," *MPR News*, March 8, 2013, http://www.mprnews.org/story/2013/03/08/health/legislative-auditor-dentist-reimbursement.

55   Senate Health, Housing, & Family Security Committee Hearing, June 12, 2007, Minnesota State University, Mankato. See Mark Fischenich, "Health Care is the Focus," *Mankato Free Press*, June 12, 2007.

56   tinyurl.com/MHP-2016-bill, p. 12.4, 2.5.

of interest, so that providers are not paid more simply for referring patients for other procedures.[57]

Also, medical providers who believe they can deliver better care or do it at a lower price, currently cannot implement those changes without needing to individually negotiate with multiple health plans to get approval and design an appropriate reimbursement system. In contrast, under the MHP, they could implement them simply by negotiating with one payer, the MHP.

The administrative simplicity of the Minnesota Health Plan will make life easier for medical providers. The MHP would be required to compensate providers in an adequate and timely manner. Providers will see significant administrative savings as they need to devote much less time to billing and collections. Uncompensated care will be virtually eliminated, ending the use of cost-shifting to recover losses.

Doctors will be able to use their best medical judgment without insurance companies looking over their shoulders the way they currently do, requiring pre-authorization for many treatments and procedures. Also, because all patients will have comprehensive coverage, doctors will no longer need to spend time and resources helping patients work around limited formularies and networks, or assisting them in getting care for services that they cannot afford. In other words, health care providers will be able to focus on what they do best—provide care—instead of pushing paperwork around or trying to cover gaps in the system.

Paying Providers under the MHP

Under the Minnesota Health Plan, as under the current system, much of the compensation would

---

57   Ibid., p. 15.7, 20.33.

likely be fee-for-service, but those fees would be based on a logical, negotiated basis, so that all services are adequately compensated (including things like phone consultations with patients), and no services would be overcompensated. Addressing the flaws with our current fee-for-service system could be accomplished quickly under the Minnesota Health Plan because the plan would not need to accept current fee schedules as a given.

The MHP would be flexible, enabling providers and the plan to seek the best form of compensation possible. If providers feel that they can provide better care to their patients, more cost-effectively, under some other payment system, they would have the opportunity to show why their idea works better. Because patients have their choice of providers under the MHP, there would be no risk of people being denied care even if providers use some form of capitation (as is currently a problem under some HMOs and managed care organizations) since a patient not receiving the care they need could switch to a different clinic or provider, an option that they currently may not have.

Salaried compensation of providers works well for many, from the Mayo Clinic to school nurses, and it would be a logical means of compensating many providers under the MHP.

Institutional providers (hospitals, nursing homes, etc.) would see payment reform as well. They would be paid through a negotiated global budget, not fee-for-service. This global budgeting would deliver huge savings because these institutions would no longer need to track every medication and every treatment they provide to each patient for billing purposes. They would be able to focus on providing high-quality care in the most efficient means possible without needing to track every service provided in order to bill each patient and their insurance plan.

Independent Medical Practices vs. Mega-Health Systems

One of the consequences of our extremely complex, bureaucratic health insurance system (the complexity of which is increased by many recent reforms such as "Accountable Care Organizations") is that small medical practices are pressured to merge with large hospital/healthcare systems.

There are some physicians who would prefer to run their own small practice, independent of any big health system. In some small communities such a doctor can significantly improve access to care. By eliminating the bureaucratic insurance system and the corresponding paperwork, and by taking away the disparities in negotiating clout between small and large practices,[58] the Minnesota Health Plan would make it significantly easier for doctors to practice independently, giving the personal care that many patients and doctors want. In addition, the MHP would end the need for doctors to spend large amounts of time getting prior authorization for procedures, and it would make interpreter services available to all providers and patients when needed. Both of these matters currently present significant challenges that doctors face when trying to remain in small, independent medical practices.[59]

A similar situation is facing many smaller hospitals who are pressured into merging with big health systems like Essentia, Mayo, and Sanford. Residents of Fairmont, Minnesota complained that the acquisition of their

---

58 Howard Bell, "Not Quite Going It Alone," *Minnesota Medicine*, November 2012, p. 14, http://www.mnmed.org/MMA/media/Minnesota-Medicine-Magazine/November-2012-web.pdf.

59 These are two of the action items recommended by a 2015 working group on independent physicians and adopted by the Minnesota Medical Association. Minnesota Medical Association Staff, personal communication, August 31, 2015.

hospital has dropped its quality of care rankings and taken away doctors.[60] The MHP would make it easier for small hospitals to remain independent if they chose to do so, again, by taking away the disparities in negotiating clout.

Assuring an Adequate Supply of Providers

Minnesota and other states produce more doctors in most medical specialties and fewer doctors in primary care than the public needs.[61] There are a variety of reasons for this, including the reality that medical students facing as much as a quarter million dollars in student loans have a strong incentive to go into specialties that pay better than primary care positions.

On top of this, many communities in Greater Minnesota have shortages of all types of health care providers, requiring people to drive long distances to get care that should be available closer to home.[62]

While there are a few modest state and federal initiatives to address shortages of general practitioners, especially in rural communities, those efforts are piecemeal. There is currently no entity responsible for creating a comprehensive strategy for meeting the need for health professionals in all Minnesota communities and simultaneously removing incentives that lead to an excess of certain types of providers.

In contrast, one of the governing principles of the MHP is a requirement that the plan ensure that there are an adequate number of health care professionals and

60 Jeremy Olson, "Fairmont Hospital Struggles after Mayo Takeover," *Star Tribune*, November 8, 2014, http://www.startribune.com/lifestyle/health/282039841.html.
61 Dennis Gottfried, "Too Many Doctors, But Too Few Primary Care Ones," *Huffington Post*, May 10, 2010, http://www.huffingtonpost.com/dr-dennis-gottfried/too-many-doctors-but-too_b_568703.html.
62 Testimony before Minnesota Senate Health, Housing, & Family Security Committee, from numerous hearings around the state in 2007 and 2008.

facilities to guarantee timely access to care in all parts of the state.[63] This could be accomplished through a variety of means, such as:

- negotiating higher reimbursements for general practitioners (and specialists where there are shortages of providers);

- providing higher pay or other incentives for those willing to work in under-served communities; or

- agreeing to pay the tuition or pay off all or part of student loans for those medical students willing go into primary care or to serve in under-served communities in Minnesota.

The shortage of certain types of providers in certain communities is a serious problem that needs attention. It won't be easy to address, but under the MHP, there will be a logical planning process to do so. In essence, this process will ultimately lead to an appropriate number of each type of provider, not an excess of some and shortage of others.

Part of the solution to both the high cost of health care and the shortage of providers is to use the full range of well-trained health professionals. For example, in dental care there are many procedures that need to be provided by a dentist and many have always been provided safely by dental hygienists. Now, Minnesota has Advanced Dental Hygiene Practitioners, mid-level professionals who are trained and qualified to provide a number of services that were formerly provided only by dentists. Increasing the number of providers able to deliver care will help address the current shortage.

---

63 tinyurl.com/MHP-2016-bill, p. 2.1.

4. Ensuring the MHP Serves the Public Good

A. Governing the MHP

The Minnesota Health Plan would be a public/private partnership, independent from the governor and state legislature. It would be governed by a board that would be required, by law, to follow the MHP principles to ensure the well-being of all Minnesotans.

Minnesota Health Board

To keep it out of partisan politics, the Minnesota Health Board would be democratically selected by county boards from around the state,[64] not appointed by state officials and not directly elected under our electoral system (which is heavily influenced by special interest money). This governance structure is modeled on the successful "County-Based Purchasing" systems that operate effectively in a number of rural Minnesota counties for delivering health care to people with disabilities or low incomes.

Eight members of the MHP's public board would be appointed by locally elected county commissioners—one from each of five regions in Greater Minnesota and three from the Metro area. Those eight board members would elect seven other board members representing health care providers and consumers.[65]

The MHP Board would negotiate provider fees and hospital budgets.[66] It would be responsible for ensuring a rational distribution of expensive technology,[67] as well as working with the University of Minnesota, other higher

---

64   Ibid., p. 14.10, 18.18.
65   Ibid., p. 14.13.
66   Ibid., p. 16.5.
67   Ibid., p. 12.23.

education institutions, and local communities to ensure sufficient providers in every community.[68]

The MHP's budget would be set through a democratic process based on health needs, not maximizing profits. This system would eliminate high CEO salaries, stock options, and bonuses based on profits, and save massive amounts of money that are currently spent on advertising, marketing, and underwriting to compete for healthy enrollees.

The board would determine premiums needed to fund the MHP, based on an individual's ability to pay.[69] Although the premiums would likely be collected by the Department of Revenue, the funds would go directly to the Minnesota Health Plan,[70] not the state, and would be used solely to pay for the Minnesota Health Plan, free from interference of legislative politics.

To ensure the MHP governing board serves the interests of patients instead of providing financial benefits for themselves or their friends, the board would have strict conflict of interest requirements.[71] The board would also be required to examine possible conflicts of interest throughout the health care system, and then work to eliminate those conflicts.[72]

Office of Health Quality and Planning

To ensure the best quality of care, it is essential to have a system in place for identifying and implementing improvements. Under the MHP, there would be an Office of Health Quality and Planning to fill that role.[73] The office would regularly make recommendations to the MHP

---

68   Ibid., p. 2.1, 12.5.
69   Ibid., p. 8.12.
70   Ibid., p. 7.5.
71   Ibid. p. 20.12.
72   Ibid., p. 15.7, 20.32.
73   Ibid., p. 19.3 - 20.11.

board on quality improvement, access to care, and public health and wellness.

Not only would the Office of Health Quality and Planning work to improve care and health outcomes, they would also play an important role in planning and budgeting. The office would investigate and make recommendations on everything from staffing levels and working conditions in health care facilities, to budget and capital expenditure needs, as well as efficiency improvements and research needs. The office would be responsible for making sure there is an adequate number of providers to meet the public needs.[74]

The MHP would also allow easier measurement of new protocols compared to existing practices. Currently, because each insurer operates with its own rules and accounting, it is difficult to make comparisons. In addition, health insurers are frequently unwilling to disclose needed data, which they consider to be trade secrets.

Embedding health quality and planning functions directly into the MHP would facilitate quicker improvements in the system. Because the Office of Health Quality and Planning would be integrated into the MHP structure, they would be able to work with other researchers and institutions to help the MHP implement their recommendations as well.

Whether proposed improvements come from the Office of Health Quality and Planning or from outside sources, good ideas could be widely adopted under the MHP without the hassle of dealing with multiple health plans, each with their own policies, governance, and financial motives.

---

74 Ibid., p. 19.27, 2.1

Ombudsman for Patient Advocacy

In any health plan, there will be disputes between patients and the system, yet patients often have little recourse. To ensure that individual patients having problems with the MHP would be well represented, there would be an Ombudsman for Patient Advocacy who would have the responsibility, authority, and resources to investigate complaints. The Ombudsman would be independent from the board, but would have the legal authority to force the MHP board to resolve problems facing patients.[75]

Auditor General for the MHP

To prevent fraud and abuse in the health care system, there would be an independent Auditor General, with the responsibility, authority, and resources to investigate, audit, and review the financial and business records related to the MHP. The auditor would regularly make recommendations to the board to improve operations and prevent waste and fraud.[76]

B. Improving Care Delivery and Integrating Public Health

Our current health care "system" is not really a system at all. It is a fragmented, inefficient, and complex patchwork of ways that people access health care. The Minnesota Health Plan would create a comprehensive, logical means of connecting people with the health care they need. The MHP would also:

- enable providers to deliver health care efficiently at convenient locations;

- integrate public health and wellness;

- assure an adequate supply of quality providers to meet the state's medical needs;[77] and

---

75   Ibid., p. 21.15, 22.33.

76   Ibid., p. 23.5.

77   As mentioned in the section: Assuring an Adequate Supply of Providers.

- facilitate evidence-based improvements in care and effectiveness.[78]

The purpose of the Minnesota Health Plan is to keep people healthy and provide care when needed. Consequently, instead of the traditional approach to health care reform, where the focus is primarily on saving money, the MHP would focus first on establishing a health care system that provides the best care. By designing a logical health care system, we will actually achieve the savings that other reforms seek.

Delivering Health Care Efficiently at Convenient Locations

The Minnesota Health Plan would ensure that providers can deliver health care at the most convenient places for people—for schoolchildren, that could mean a school nurse in every school, and for adults, small clinics at large workplaces and retail centers around the state.[79]

School Nurses

School nurses would provide general medical care as needed, including delivery of routine vaccinations. To understand what a difference this makes, compare the way we deliver flu shots to children now and how we. could do so under the MHP.

Currently, for parents who want their children to get their annual flu vaccination, first they need to make an appointment, then they need to take time off work, go to their children's school(s), take them out of class, drive them to a clinic to get the shot, return them to school, then return to work. This is an incredibly inefficient and, therefore, expensive means of delivering vaccinations. As a result, less than 60% of students receive an annual

---

78   As mentioned above in the section: Office of Health Quality and Planning.

79   tinyurl.com/MHP-2016-bill, p. 17.2.

influenza vaccination,[80] despite the Center for Disease Control's (CDC) recommendation that everyone (six months or older) receive such a vaccination each year.[81]

In contrast, under the MHP, with a nurse in every school, delivering flu shots to students would require nothing more than sending consent forms to parents and providing the nurse with sufficient vaccines. With far less cost, far less disruption of the school day, and far less disruption of parents' work days, we could deliver vaccinations to significantly more young people than we do now.

Likewise, school nurses could do much to prevent teenage pregnancy and sexually-transmitted infections. Public health studies show that about half of high school seniors are sexually active.[82] Giving students the option of turning to a school nurse would be far more effective than hoping those students find a way to get to a family planning clinic.

Health Care Where People Work

Some large employers currently have medical clinics or nurses available at the workplace for the convenience and well-being of their employees and to save money. Under the MHP any location where there are numerous employees, whether a downtown office building or a large shopping mall, might be well served by having a small medical clinic on-site.

---

80   The Centers for Disease Control and Prevention (CDC) reports that 59.3% of Minnesota children aged 6 months—17 years received an influenza vaccination in 2010-11. See CDC, "2010-11 State, Regional, and National Vaccination Report I," http://www.cdc.gov/flu/fluvaxview/reportshtml/reporti1011/reporti/index.html.
81   "Everyone 6 months of age and older should get a flu vaccine every season." See CDC, "Key Facts About Seasonal Flu Vaccine," http://www.cdc.gov/flu/protect/keyfacts.htm.
82   Child Trends Data Bank, "Percentage of Students in Grades 9 through 12 Who Report They Are Sexually Active, by Grade and Gender, 2013," http://www.childtrends.org/wp-content/uploads/2012/07/23_Fig3.jpg.

Through a comprehensive health system like the MHP, changes like this can occur relatively quickly. Contrast this with the current system, where no insurer is likely to place a nurse in a large office building for the sake of those workers, when only a small percentage of those workers are members of their particular health plan.

By making everything from mental health services to flu vaccinations easily available and with no fee or copayment, we can increase efficiency, reduce the cost of administering the services, and help keep people healthy—the goal of any responsible health care system.

Integrating Public Health and Wellness into the System

As Ben Franklin declared, "an ounce of prevention is worth a pound of cure." People understand that it is often less expensive to prevent a problem than to fix that problem after it has occurred.[83] Prevention and early intervention can deliver huge improvements in health, and in some cases, such as chemical dependency treatment and family planning services, it can save money as well.

Under our current "non-system," investments in public health and wellness are afterthoughts that require political will; they take dollars from other, often unrelated, public needs in order to invest in health and wellness. In a true health care *system,* such as the Minnesota Health Plan, there would be more investment in public health and wellness, especially in those instances where the investments save money through reduced medical costs. The Minnesota Health Plan also

---

83 There are many situations in which prevention and early detection efforts do *not* save money to the health system because the treatment may cost more than ignoring the problem might have cost. However, the primary goal of a health care system is not to save money; it is to keep people healthy, so prevention is important even in cases where it might cost more.

has the benefit of scale—because the MHP covers the entire population, it can finance public health initiatives for the entire state. It can also target specific segments of the community to meet specific needs such as HIV prevention for at-risk populations, or programs aimed at seniors, young people, farm communities, or people in the core cities.

In Minnesota, like many other states, there are already a number of public health programs designed to reduce the number of people who smoke, to encourage exercise, to prevent obesity, etc. However, those programs are usually available only in select communities during specific time periods. They are frequently "pilot projects," not ongoing initiatives available to all. Even if those public health programs improve health, and even if they save money, public health agencies struggle to find funding to operate them. The MHP is responsible for saving money and keeping people healthy, so it would logically incorporate public health programs into the overall system. Because the MHP is in charge of the entire system, effective public health initiatives would make sense both from health and economic perspectives.

5. Economics of the MHP

One of the most frequent questions that people ask when they hear about a universal health care system like the Minnesota Health Plan is, "How much will it cost?" They know health care is already too expensive in the United States, and wonder how much *more* it will cost to cover more people for more things.

Yet despite covering additional people and providing comprehensive benefits for everyone, numerous studies and the actual experience of Medicare show that a health care system like the Minnesota Health Plan is actually less expensive than our current system due to administrative savings, more efficient delivery of care, savings from price negotiations, and other factors.

The clearest evidence of this counter-intuitive reality is a comparison with other nations.

The U.S. is the only wealthy, industrialized nation on the planet that doesn't provide universal health care,[84] the only one where millions of people are uninsured and millions more are under-insured, and yet we spend almost twice as much as any other industrialized nation pays for care, whether measured per capita or as a percentage of the GDP.[85]

Cost studies of proposals that replace the multi-payer health insurance model with a single plan to pay medical bills—often referred to as "single-payer" systems—have consistently concluded that a single-payer plan will cover

---

84   David de Ferranti (former Vice President of the World Bank) and Julio Frenk (Dean of the Harvard School of Public Health), "Toward University Health Coverage," *New York Times*, April 6, 2012, http://www.nytimes.com/2012/04/06/opinion/toward-universal-health-coverage.html?_r=3.
85   OECD, "Total Expenditure on Health Per capita," June 30, 2014, http://www.oecd-ilibrary.org/social-issues-migration-health/total-expenditure-on-health-per-capita_20758480-table2.

all people at less cost than the current system.[86] These studies show that we can cover everyone and still save money for both individuals and businesses. Under one study of a generic universal health care system similar to the MHP, a median income ($60,000/year) Minnesota family[87] would save about $3,500 per year, and a business that offers employee health benefits would save an average of $1,200 per employee.[88]

This result was reached by the Lewin Group, a research firm owned by United Health Group, the nation's largest health insurance company. The Lewin Group is clearly not biased in favor of a single-payer system, because such a health care system would displace the business of its parent company. Lewin has conducted cost studies of such proposals in Minnesota, Colorado, and other states, showing net savings.[89]

---

86 See report from The Lewin Group on Colorado, "Technical Assessment of Health Care Reform Proposals," August 20, 2007, http://tinyurl.com/Colorado-2007Lewin. See also Amy Lange, "Beyond the Affordable Care Act: An Economic Analysis of a Unified System of Health Care for Minnesota," *Growth & Justice*, March 2012, http://growthandjustice.org/publication/BeyondACA.pdf, and Ida Hellander, "Single Payer System Cost?" *Physicians for a National Health Program*, July 2013, http://www.pnhp.org/facts/single-payer-system-cost.
87 United States Census Bureau, "State & County QuickFacts: Minnesota," last revised September 30, 2015, http://quickfacts.census.gov/qfd/states/27000.html.
88 Amy Lange, "Beyond the Affordable Care Act: An Economic Analysis of a Unified System of Health Care for Minnesota," *Growth & Justice*, March 2012, p. 22, 24, http://growthandjustice.org/publication/BeyondACA.pdf.
89 The Colorado study analyzed four health reform proposals. Three of the four proposals cost more, yet each of them left many people uninsured. Only the single payer proposal covered everyone, yet it was the only one that reduced health care spending. See report from Lewin Group, "Technical Assessment of Health Care Reform Proposals," August 20, 2007, http://tinyurl.com/Colorado-2007Lewin. For the Lewin Group's Minnesota study, see John Sheils and Megan Cole, "Cost and Economic Impact Analysis of a Single-Payer Plan in Minnesota," *Growth & Justice*, March 27, 2012, http://www.growthandjustice.org/images/uploads/LEWIN.Final_Report_FINAL_DRAFT.pdf.

While these results are extremely positive, most of the studies analyzed only two or three financial impacts of the plans:

(a) the additional cost of covering more people,

(b) the administrative savings from elimination of insurance costs of a multi-payer system, and

(c) the benefits of bulk purchasing.

Although the Minnesota Health Plan is similar to those single-payer proposals, it offers a complete health care system, not just a different financing system. As a result, the Minnesota Health Plan would provide significant additional savings from aspects of the plan which were outside the scope of other single payer proposals and previous cost studies.

A. Overview of Cost Impacts

When comparing the total costs of health care between the Minnesota Health Plan and our current system, there are some elements of the MHP that save money, some that increase costs, and some secondary factors that would either mitigate increases or result in additional savings.

> **Factors in the MHP that would reduce costs include**: administrative efficiency and elimination of the vast insurance bureaucracy, bulk purchasing of drugs and medical supplies at lower, negotiated prices, allocation of medical infrastructure based on regional needs, use of annual budgets for health care facilities (replacing the costly task of itemizing, billing, and collecting individual expenses for each patient), and fairly negotiated provider fees.

> **Factors that would increase costs include**: increased use of services due to universal coverage and to comprehensive benefits without out-of-pocket costs.

There are also some **secondary factors that
would mitigate increases in cost from higher
utilization** or result in additional savings, such
as the increased use of preventive services and
early intervention. These services reduce costly
emergency room and hospitalization expenses,
and prevent conditions from becoming more acute.
Some of these savings come in economic sectors
outside of health care, e.g., chemical dependency
treatment can reduce criminal justice and human
services costs.

B. Increasing Efficiency by Reducing Bureaucracy

Health insurers spend significant amounts of money
on expenses that do not treat or care for patients, such
as designing policies, marketing, sales, billing and
collections, and more. Administrative costs of the health
care system in the United States are as much as 31 cents of
every dollar spent on health care.[90]

Billing and Insurance-Related Costs

The patchwork system of billing and paying for our
health care is extremely inefficient. Health care providers
have extensive administrative overhead to bill and collect
payment from dozens of different health plans and a
multitude of policies from each plan.

The insurance-related administrative savings come from
each end of every financial transaction. Not only would
the MHP save money on the insurance company end, but
also from providers, employers, and patients. Clinics and
hospitals currently have multiple billing and accounting
clerks to handle the billing of dozens of different health

---

90 Steffie Woolhandler, Terry Campbell, and David U. Himmelstein,
"Costs of Health Care Administration in the United States and Canada,"
New England Journal of Medicine 349 (August 21, 2003), pp. 768-775, http://
www.nejm.org/doi/full/10.1056/NEJMsa022033#t=article.

plans at different rates for each procedure for thousands of patients.[91] In order for hospital and nursing home billing offices to bill patients and health plans for each treatment and expense, nurses and other medical staff need to spend time itemizing treatments and procedures to send to the billing office, which is separate from the recording they do for the patient's medical charts.

Each health plan requires different deductibles and co-payments for their members. Because not all patients are able to pay, billing and collection costs are high, and providers shift costs to other payers. Also, many providers need clerks to counsel patients on which services are covered and help them try to find coverage for a procedure.

The complexities don't end there. Each plan has different administrative requirements which often require providers to track and resubmit bills that are initially rejected or lost in the shuffle. Unfortunately, physicians report the administrative burden is getting worse.[92]

The MHP would virtually eliminate uncompensated care, reducing subsequent cost shifting as well as collection costs. Also, by ending health plan administrative requirements designed to harass clinics into writing off some claims,[93]

---

91 "Administrative costs accounted for 25 percent of hospital spending in the United States, more than twice the proportion seen in Canada and Scotland," See David U. Himmelstein, et al., "A Comparison of Hospital Administrative Costs in Eight Nations: U.S. Costs Exceed All Others by Far," *The Commonwealth Fund*, September 8, 2014, http://www.commonwealthfund. org/publications/in-the-literature/2014/sep/hospital-administrative-costs.
92 "More than 75 percent of physicians and administrators reported that the administrative burden of interacting with a health plan increased significantly or increased slightly in the past two years." See Lawrence P. Casalino, "What Are the Costs to Physicians of Administrative Complexity in Their Interactions with Payers?" *Findings Brief: Changes in Health Care Financing & Organization (HCFO)*, 13:2 (March 2010), p. 2, https://www. academyhealth.org/files/publications/HCFOMarchFindingsBrief.pdf.
93 One of the tactics that some insurance companies use to deny legitimate

the MHP would make life much simpler for physicians and other providers and increase their bottom line.

By having only the Minnesota Health Plan pay all of the bills, all at uniform, negotiated rates, and avoiding the need to bill each patient, the MHP would significantly reduce administrative and billing costs for both the plan and providers.

The simplification of the billing and insurance-related (BIR) administrative system generates perhaps the biggest savings of any aspect of health care reform. A 2014 study of the savings from a simple payment system like the MHP shows savings totaling almost 15% of the cost of our entire health care system.[94] With 2016 health spending in Minnesota projected to be over $50 billion,[95] that means savings of over $7 billion per year. Seven billion dollars in savings can pay for a lot of health care for a lot of people!

---

claims occurs when a doctor that they have "credentialed" moves to a new clinic. The insurer requires the physician to be re-credentialed by them at the new clinic, even though there has been no change in the doctor's qualifications or experience. The insurance companies often take two to three months to complete this re-credentialing. During that waiting period, any patients the physician treats will not be compensated by the insurer. Personal communication from three different medical clinics.

94 "BIR costs in the U.S. health care system totaled approximately $471 billion in 2012. This includes $70 billion in physician practices, $74 billion in hospitals, an estimated $94 billion in settings providing other health services and supplies, $198 billion in private insurers, and $35 billion in public insurers. Compared to simplified financing, $375 billion, or 80%, represents the added BIR costs of the current multi-payer system... A simplified financing system in the U.S. could result in cost savings exceeding $350 billion annually, nearly 15% of health care spending." See Aliya Jiwani, et al., "Billing and Insurance-Related Administrative Costs in United States' Health Care: Synthesis of Micro-Costing Evidence," *BMC Health Services Research* 14:556 (2014), http://bmchealthservres.biomedcentral.com/articles/10.1186/s12913-014-0556-7.

95 $50.7 billion in 2016 projections from the Minnesota Department of Health. "Minnesota Health Care Spending and Projections, 2013," March 2016, Table 4, p. 26, http://www.health.state.mn.us/divs/hpsc/hep/publications/costs/healthspending2016.pdf.

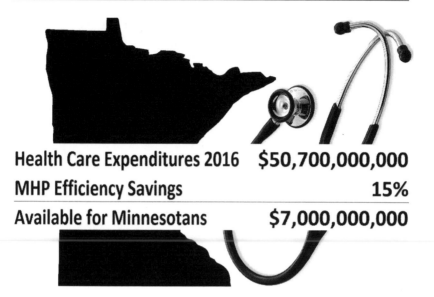

Health Care Expenditures 2016 $50,700,000,000

MHP Efficiency Savings   15%

Available for Minnesotans $7,000,000,000

Elimination of Underwriting

The administrative costs in our current system from insurance company underwriting are significant. Under the MHP, the costs of underwriting by insurance companies to select healthier people and reject sicker, more costly people—and the cost-shifting caused by it—would be eliminated. Underwriting by insurance companies is justified by the fact that it makes health care less expensive for healthier people. The opposite is true as well: underriting makes health care more expensive (and consequently more difficult to access) for the people who need it most—those who are older, sicker, and have more health problems. The complications resulting from their difficulty in accessing care ironically contribute to the high costs of the overall health care system, which drive up costs for even twhe healthiest people who are supposed to be the beneficiaries of underwriting.

Although the Affordable Care Act (ACA) was supposed to eliminate underwriting, insurance companies found other ways of cherry-picking healthier customers.

"Cherry-Picking of Patients Under the ACA

Because there is no way to remove the financial incentive insurers have to push (encourage) people with expensive health needs to switch insurance plans, health plans find other ways to make the financial gains they previously made from underwriting and denying coverage to people with preexisting conditions.

An example of how insurers are now pushing sicker patients away is by declaring certain generic medications used to treat serious, chronic conditions as "non-preferred." This makes them more costly to the patient than the "preferred" drugs, discouraging patients with those expensive conditions from choosing those insurance plans.

"Many patients are now encountering much higher co-pays for generic drugs that have been designated 'non-preferred' by their insurers… For some diseases, in fact, many insurers have no 'preferred' generic medicines, effectively rendering the diseases themselves 'non-preferred.'"[96]

While "cherry-picking" of the healthiest people through underwriting or denying coverage to those with preexisting conditions is now illegal, insurers know that by making things more expensive or more difficult for people with chronic conditions, they can accomplish the same financial gain. People who require medications to manage some of these "non-preferred" health conditions will avoid selecting an insurance plan that does not cover their medication or places the medication in a higher cost tier.

---

96 Gerry Oster and A. Mark Fendrick, "Is All "Skin in the Game" Fair Fame? The Problem with "Non-Preferred" Generics." *American Journal of Managed Care*, 20:9 (2014), pp. 693-695, http://www.ajmc.com/journals/issue/2014/2014-vol20-n9/is-all-skin-in-the-game-fair-game-the-problem-with-non-preferred-generics.

*Health plans may attempt to defend this practice by
claiming they need to do so because of the high cost
of some new drugs. "The demand that patients pay a
larger share of their drug costs, however, is not limited
to expensive new medicines. In fact, many patients are
now facing substantially higher co-pays for various
generic drugs that their insurers have designated
'non-preferred,' often including those recommended
as first-line treatment in evidence-based guidelines for
hypertension, diabetes, epilepsy, schizophrenia, migraine
headache, osteoporosis, Parkinson's disease, and human
immunodeficiency virus (HIV)."[97]*

*One health plan placed a diabetes medication,
Metformin, in the more costly "non-preferred" tier. A
price check at Walmart and Walgreens[98] shows that
this prescription can be purchased by those without
insurance coverage for only $4 for a 30-day supply.*

*The health plan is not making this medication more
expensive to its members because the drug is expensive,
but to avoid the significantly higher cost of insuring
people with type 2 diabetes.[99]*

---

97 Ibid.

98 See "Convenient Prescription Refills from $4," *Walmart*, http://
www.walmart.com/cp/1078664, and "Value-Priced Medication
List," *Walgreens*, March 2012, http://www.walgreens.com/images/
psc/pdf/PSC_2_0_VPG_List_FINAL_32312.pdf.

99 According to a study by G. Bruno, et al., "Direct costs are
4-fold higher in diabetic than in non-diabetic people." See G.
Bruno, et al., "Direct Costs in Diabetic and Non Diabetic People:
The Population-Based Turin Study, Italy." *Nutrition, Metabolism,
and Cardiovascular Disease*, 22:8 (August 2012), pp. 684-90, http://
www.ncbi.nlm.nih.gov/pubmed/21907553. According to a study
by the American Diabetes Association, "People with diagnosed
diabetes, on average, have medical expenditures approximately
2.3 times higher than what expenditures would be in the absence
of diabetes." See the American Diabetes Association, "The Cost of
Diabetes," http://www.diabetes.org/advocacy/news-events/cost-of-
diabetes.html.

Under the Minnesota Health Plan, with a single plan covering everyone, there is no underwriting expense and no game-playing aimed at attracting healthy, low cost patients to one plan, or pushing unhealthy, expensive patients towards other plans.

This is important both for patient health and economic reasons.

Eliminating Direct-to-Consumer Drug Marketing

Direct-to-consumer marketing of pharmaceuticals costs Minnesotans over $100 million per year.[100] The MHP aims to end such advertising by paying for all drugs except those marketed directly to consumers in Minnesota.[101]

As a result, if the drug companies chose to continue such advertising in Minnesota, their customers would be responsible for paying for those drugs out of pocket, when competitors' drugs would be paid for by the MHP. In order not to lose customers, the drug companies would likely stop marketing directly to consumers here. Among other benefits, Minnesotans would see an end to those irritating "ask your doctor" drug advertisements on television.

By effectively ending that advertising, the MHP would have a negotiating advantage in seeking additional savings because drug manufacturers would have over $100 million in lower costs, being spared the significant expense of that advertising.

In addition, drug manufacturers only spend money on advertising because it increases the demand for expensive drugs. Eliminating that advertising decreases patient demand for costly drugs which are often not the most

100 Stephen Schondelmeyer, Pharm.D., Ph.D. (Professor and Head, Department of Pharmaceutical Care & Health Systems, University of Minnesota), personal communication, 2015.
101 tinyurl.com/MHP-2016-bill, p. 6.20, 1.20.

appropriate, creating further savings of well over $400 million per year.[102]

Marketing Costs for Insurance Plans

Currently, health plans spend many millions of dollars on marketing to attract customers from their competitors. Because the MHP would cover everyone, it would not need to advertise for more customers. If the MHP were to spend money on marketing, those advertising dollars would be devoted to public health and wellness promotion, not recruiting more business.

Consumer Time and Expense

On top of all of these costs for providers and payers, employers and individuals also spend significant time and expense shopping for an appropriate health plan and negotiating rates (often annually), then throughout the year figuring out which services are covered and which providers are in network, as well as trying to decipher various charges before paying bills or contesting unfair or inappropriate ones. Obviously, although the costs of these tasks are not usually counted as health care expenditures, they have a very real impact on employers and individuals. The MHP would eliminate these unnecessary burdens.

Furthermore, patients are not always able to use a logical, nearby, health facility because it is not in their provider's network. Sometimes this requires significant additional travel and time costs for patients and families. The MHP would avoid such costs by having one statewide, all-inclusive network.

---

102 A study by the Kaiser Family Foundation found that "every $1 the pharmaceutical industry spent on DTC advertising in [2000] yielded an additional $4.20 in drug sales." See Kaiser Family Foundation, "Impact of Direct-to-Consumer Advertising on Prescription Drug Spending," June 10, 2003, http://kff.org/health-costs/report/impact-of-direct-to-consumer-advertising-on-prescription-drug-spending/.

C. Better Budgeting and Pricing

Price Negotiations for Medical Services

Our health care system overcharges for many medical products and services, and pays too little for others.

For medical treatments and services, health plans negotiate lower rates for people in their plan, so their members pay significantly less for those services (even when factoring in both health plan payments and member co-payments) than uninsured patients do. Under the MHP, rates for all patients would be negotiated by the plan, which would result in lower prices due to its strong bargaining clout.

Currently, there is widespread variation in prices, based on the provider, the payer, and the patient. A 2013 Time Magazine special report on health care pricing[103] by Steven Brill drew national attention to the wide disparities in costs, which were already apparent to many of those unable to pay off medical debt. Brill gave numerous examples such as hospital patients being charged $18 for each Accu-Chek diabetes test strip which he reported were available on Amazon for about 55 cents each.

A December 2015 paper by Zack Cooper of Yale University reported that hospital prices for a basic knee replacement ranged from about $3,400 at the lowest price hospital to about $55,800 for the same procedure at the highest price hospital.[104]

---

103   Steven Brill, "Bitter Pill: Why Medical Bills Are Killing Us," *Time Magazine Special Report*, Feb. 20, 2013, http://healthland.time.com/2013/02/20/ bitter-pill-why-medical-bills-are-killing-us/print/, also available at http:// www.uta.edu/faculty/story/2311/Misc/2013,2,26,MedicalCostsDemandAndG reed.pdf.
104   Zack Cooper, et al., "The Price Ain't Right? Hospital Prices and Health Spending on the Privately Insured," *Health Care Pricing Project*, December 2015, p. 48, http://www.healthcarepricingproject.org/sites/default/files/ pricing_variation_manuscript_0.pdf. See also Kevin Quealy and Sanger-

A sixteen hundred percent variation in pricing is evidence of a dysfunctional market! Replacing this irrational pricing system with fairly negotiated prices would likely result in large savings. Under Medicare's price negotiation system, procedures that have a wide range in pricing in the insurance market have a much narrower variation under Medicare, with less than a two to one differential across the country.[105]

For medical equipment, supplies, and prescriptions, negotiated savings would be significant as well. Prescription drug pricing in the United States is handled in a complex, secretive, and uncompetitive manner that includes financial kickbacks.

As a result, Americans pay significantly more than people in other nations for pharmaceuticals—about 40% more than the next highest spending country.[106] The pharmaceutical companies are *not* selling their drugs at a loss in other countries; they sell them at prices where they make a profit. They simply make much more money in the US because of the anti-competitive, convoluted pricing scheme here. In fact, in 2013 the pharmaceutical companies had an average profit margin of 18%, and the

---

Katz, Margot, "The Experts Were Wrong About the Best Places for Better and Cheaper Health Care," *New York Times*, December 15, 2015, http://www.nytimes.com/interactive/2015/12/15/upshot/the-best-places-for-better-cheaper-health-care-arent-what-experts-thought.html?_r=4. "The least costly price in the study for the simplest type of knee replacement was only about $3,400. The most expensive one was about $55,800."

105 "[W]ithin the regulated Medicare reimbursement system, the hospital with the highest reimbursement for lower limb MRIs in the nation is paid 1.87 times the least reimbursed." Zack Cooper, et al., "The Price Ain't Right? Hospital Prices and Health Spending on the Privately Insured," *Health Care Pricing Project*, December 2015, p. 3, http://www.healthcarepricingproject. org/sites/default/files/pricing_variation_manuscript_0.pdf.

106 Valerie Paris, OECD, "Why do Americans spend so much on pharmaceuticals?" *PBS NewsHour*, February 7, 2014, http://www.pbs.org/newshour/updates/americans-spend-much-pharmaceuticals.

largest was Pfizer, with an enormous 42% profit margin.[107]

Likewise, the radical difference in drug prices paid by the Veterans Administration, which negotiates prices, and Medicare, which does not, is well known. Among the top 20 drugs prescribed for seniors, the median difference between the lowest Medicare price and the lowest VA price was 58%.[108] By negotiating fair prices for drugs and other medical goods and services, and doing so for all patients, there would be great savings under the MHP.

For pharmaceutical purchasing, not only would there be savings from negotiated drug prices, but by handling all of the drug purchasing, the MHP would eliminate the costly cut taken by Pharmacy Benefit Managers (PBMs), generating additional savings.[109] "PBMs are simply middlemen. They don't sell drug products. PBMs don't see patients. They don't provide patient care," according to Michael Deninger, a pharmacist who writes about pharmaceutical pricing.[110]

Salaries and reimbursement for providers may go down in some cases due to negotiations, but may increase for others. For example, there is a shortage of psychiatrists

---

107   Catherine D. DeAngelis, "Big Pharma Profits and the Public Loses," *The Milbank Quarterly* 94:1 (2016), pp. 30-33, http://www.milbank.org/the-milbank-quarterly/search-archives/article/4074/big-pharma-profits-and-the-public-loses.
108   Families USA, "No Bargain: Medicare Drug Plans Deliver High Prices," January 2007, Families USA Publication No. 07-101, p. 4, https://web.archive.org/web/20130827191450/http://www.familiesusa.org/assets/pdfs/no-bargain-medicare-drug.pdf or a summary is available at: http://consumersunion.org/pub/pdf/no-bargain.pdf.
109   PBMs may add to the cost of drugs almost as much as pharmacies do, purely in an administrative purchasing role, "without having employees in the trenches caring for patients, without any investment in brick and mortar stores, and with inventory and equipment needed to actually dispense prescriptions." Michael Deninger, "Examining Medicare Part D Transparency," *The Thriving Pharmacist*, May 12, 2015, http://www.thethrivingpharmacist.com/2015/05/12/examining-medicare-part-d-transparency.
110   Michael Deninger, "The King is Naked," *The Thriving Pharmacist*, December 21, 2015, www.thethrivingpharmacist.com/2015/12/21/the-king-is-naked.

and primary care providers, especially in small rural communities. The MHP may compensate at a higher rate to provide incentives to practice in those specialties or communities. The MHP may also choose to increase compensation rates for primary care providers so that doctors can spend the time necessary to address their patients' needs, rather than racing from patient to patient.

The pricing of medical goods and services is a root cause of our out-of-control health care costs. The fair, negotiated pricing and payment system under the MHP would get to the core of this problem quickly and effectively.

Global Budgeting for Hospitals and Nursing Homes

Under the MHP, there would be a negotiated annual budget for each hospital and nursing home. Consequently, those facilities would eliminate the costly task of itemizing individual expenses for each patient, as well as billing and collecting at the different rates paid by each insurance company. This would allow the facilities to focus on delivering care, not tracking expenses and billing for each patient.

Maryland began a five-year experiment with global budgets for hospitals in 2014.[111] Under the plan, hospitals are paid a global budget each year, instead of paying for each individual patient and each service provided. The first year savings were "more than $100 million, and hospital readmissions were down at a rate faster than the national average," according to the Maryland Hospital Association.[112]

111   Andis Robeznieks, "Global Budgets Pushing Maryland Hospitals to Target Population Health," *Modern Healthcare*, December 6, 2014, http://www.modernhealthcare.com/article/20141206/MAGAZINE/312069983.
112   Audie Cornish, "In Maryland, A Change in How Hospitals Are Paid Boosts Public Health," *NPR News*, October 23, 2015, http://www.npr.org/sections/health-shots/2015/10/23/451212483/in-maryland-a-change-in-how-hospitals-are-paid-boosts-public-health.

To understand the significance of these savings, consider an analogy. If public schools were funded the way we fund hospitals:

> Each teacher would need to spend significant time on a daily basis calculating how much time they spent with each student, along with the amount of supplies each student consumed. Then, the school would need to allocate a portion of janitorial costs, facility costs, and administrative overhead to each student.
>
> Also, the school would need a billing office to bill each student's family or their "education insurance plan." However, each family's plan would pay for different services at different rates, with different co-payments. Not all families would have "education insurance," and many families would struggle to pay. As a result, the school would spend more resources to collect the payments and cost-shift unpaid expenses to other students.

Funding our schools in this manner would cost much more and absorb a significant portion of each teacher's time, while doing nothing to improve the quality of education. We would never want to fund schools the way we fund hospitals.

Ending Exorbitant Health Plan Executive Compensation

The MHP would also end excessive salaries for health insurance company executives. In their place, the top executive compensation for the Minnesota Health Plan would be capped.[113] Several Minnesota non-profit health

---

113 tinyurl.com/MHP-2016-bill, p. 13.20.

plans have executive salaries over $1 million/year, not to mention the even more obscene salaries paid at for-profit health plans such as United Health Care. A former United Health Care CEO ended up with over $800 million in stock, even *after* he was forced to pay back over $600 million in stock options,[114] plus he was given a severance package worth $286 million.[115]

D. Delivery System Planning and Innovation

Reduction in Excess Capacity of Medical Facilities

The current health care system is wasteful, not only in denying appropriate care, but also in creating excessive capacity in certain costly equipment such as MRIs and radiation therapy technology. For example, radiation therapy clinics can cost several million dollars to construct, yet there are two located directly across the street from each other in Maplewood, Minnesota, each run by different providers hoping to get lucrative business. Under the MHP, the board would ensure facilities are built where needed,[116] not where one provider is hoping to attract patients from a competitor.

Care Coordination

The MHP would enable all Minnesotans to have care coordination,[117] at the clinic they choose. There are costs (which would be covered by the MHP) but also savings from care coordination. Care coordinators can

---

114   As part of a settlement with the Securities and Exchange Commission., Eric Dash, "Former Chief Will Forfeit $418 Million," *New York Times,* December 7, 2007, http://www.nytimes.com/2007/12/07/business/07options.html.

115   "William McGuire, who served as UnitedHealth's CEO from 1991 to 2006, collected $286 million when he retired." See "Top 10 Largest CEO Severance Packages of the Past Decade," *Forbes,* http://www.forbes.com/pictures/ehii45khf/william-mcguire-at-unitedhealth-286-million.

116   tinyurl.com/MHP-2016-bill, p. 12.23.

117   Ibid., p. 6.24.

work with patients on health improvement, make sure immunizations are up to date, and ensure that patients know where to turn for appropriate care. In addition, by having a care coordinator who keeps track of medical test results, there would be fewer repeat tests on patients by doctors who were unaware that the tests had already been performed.

Using the Full Range of Health Professionals

The MHP would take advantage of the wide variety of health professionals to provide care and treatment in an efficient and cost effective manner. For example, there are some medical services where a physician assistant may provide better care than a physician at a lower cost.[118] Allowing qualified professionals—such as advanced practice nurses, physical therapists, or dental hygienists— to use the skills in which they have been trained is less expensive than using overqualified providers to deliver the same services. By recognizing the qualifications (and limitations) of each type of practitioner, and reimbursing them for the services they are trained to give, the MHP would save money by appropriate use of the full range of health care professionals.

One All-Inclusive Provider Network

Provider networks are for the benefit of health insurance plans, so they can compete with each other by offering different networks of doctors and hospitals. Without insurance companies in the MHP, there is no need for limited networks. Patients can choose their providers.[119]

This elimination of many overlapping provider networks reduces confusion (about who is "in-network" vs. who is

---

118 Dr. Thomas H. Bracken, Onamia, MN, letter to the editor, *Star Tribune*, January 18, 2009, http://www.startribune.com/opinion/letters/37743134.html?page=all&prepage=2&c=y#continue.
119 tinyurl.com/MHP-2016-bill, p. 1.22, 4.25.

"out-of-network"), and reduces administrative expenses for both providers and patients. It also reduces costs from transporting patients to more distant providers simply because those providers are "in-network."

Savings from Improved Medical Data Interoperability

Both patients and providers are frequently frustrated by the inability to have the patient's medical record available to the provider treating the patient. Our fragmented, inefficient health care system has led to fragmented, inefficient data-sharing in Minnesota. The multiple health plans and provider networks all make massive investments in data systems that are not compatible with those of competitors. Nor is there a financial incentive for them to do so.[120]

The 2015 Minnesota Health Care Financing Task Force heard testimony about how doctors, pharmacists, and hospitals will often have differing records about the prescriptions a patient is taking. In an age of instantaneous, world-wide data sharing capabilities, the Task Force was told that when providers receive electronic medical records on medication history, lab results, or care summaries from other providers outside of their health system, those electronic records must usually be integrated into their own system by fax, scan, or pdf.[121]

Under a single, universal health system, information about patients' health needs can easily follow them and be instantly available when needed. Not only would there be large economic savings from having the Minnesota Health Plan implement a fully interoperable system, but

---

120 Robert Pear, "Tech Rivalries Impede Digital Medical Record Sharing," *New York Times*, May 6, 2015, http://www.nytimes.com/2015/05/27/us/ electronic-medical-record-sharing-is-hurt-by-business-rivalries.html?_r=1. 121 Minnesota Health Care Financing Task Force, "Health Care Delivery Design & Sustainability," October 24, 2015, p. 5, http://mn.gov/dhs/images/ workgroup1-presentation-10-23.pdf.

there are also significant safety and health improvements when doctors can know what medications the patient is taking and learn of other health conditions of which they need to be aware in order to best treat the patient.

Eliminating Conflicts of Interest

The MHP board would be required to study potential conflicts of interest in the health care system and then work to prevent them,[122] including conflicts when there are incentives for providers to order additional tests or procedures at facilities in which they have a financial stake. Also, addressing conflicts of interest related to gifts from pharmaceutical and medical device manufacturers will remove the incentive for providers to select more expensive drugs.[123]

E. Changes in Care Utilization

The MHP controls costs by cutting waste, not by denying care to patients.

Timely and Appropriate Use of Medical Care

Because of the way our current system is designed, many people end up using costly emergency room care for routine medical needs. For example, Minnesotans make almost 33,000 emergency room visits annually for dental problems,[124] which emergency rooms are not equipped to handle. The MHP would avoid inappropriate use of emergency care by giving every Minnesotan access to regular medical (and dental) office visits and care.

---

122 tinyurl.com/MHP-2016-bill, p. 15.7, 15.9, 20.12, 20.32.

123 John Dudley Miller, "Study Affirms Pharma's Influence on Physicians," *Journal of the National Cancer Institute* 99:15 (2007), pp. 1148-1150, http://jnci.oxfordjournals.org/content/99/15/1148.full.

124 From 2007 to 2010, 131,914 patients were treated in hospital emergency rooms for non-traumatic oral and dental conditions. See MN Department of Health, "Minnesota Oral Health Plan 2013-2018: Advancing Optimal Oral Health for All Minnesotans," January 2013, p. 13, http://www.health.state. mn.us/oralhealth/pdfs/StatePlan2013.pdf.

The MHP would also reduce emergency room use through a 24-hour/day public health nurse phone line to help people determine whether their medical situation merits a visit to their doctor.[125] In addition, every Minnesotan would have access to 24-hour urgent care clinics co-located with emergency rooms to avoid unnecessary emergency room use.[126]

The current health care system is backwards in the manner it provides health care. For many people without health insurance, and even for many who are covered, the current system does not work to prevent illness or intervene early. It frequently does not deliver care until the situation becomes acute, when it costs far more to treat.

Health care reform should not focus on *reducing* utilization, especially when many people already do not get the care they should have. The goal should be to focus on *appropriate* utilization. Americans visit doctors and hospitals less often than people in many other countries.[127] Over-utilization is not the problem we need to focus on; appropriate utilization is. For example, we need to get people *in* for routine dental care, and keep them *out* of emergency rooms for dental pain.

Because the MHP would be responsible for paying for lifelong health care, it is in the plan's best interest to keep everyone as healthy as possible. Keeping people healthy is not only the moral imperative of a health plan, it is also the fiscally responsible means of delivering health care.

---

125   tinyurl.com/MHP-2016-bill, p. 19.1.
126   Ibid., p. 19.2.
127   "OECD Health Statistics 2014—Frequently Requested Data," see "Health Care Activities" charts, http://www.oecd.org/els/health-systems/oecd-health-statistics-2014-frequently-requested-data.htm. On downloaded chart, under Health Care Activities, see "Doctor Consultations," "Hospital Discharge Rates," "Average Length of Stay," etc.

The Myth of "Skin in the Game" & Appropriate Utilization

One of the myths about health care costs is that patients will get wasteful, unnecessary care unless they have "skin in the game," meaning they need to have significant co-payments and deductibles. It is said that we all want the "Cadillac" treatment with the best, most expensive care.

In reality, while most people like their doctors, few people want to visit them, few people want to undergo medical tests, few people enjoy a colonoscopy or knee replacement surgery.

Co-pays and deductibles are a poor means of encouraging people to get appropriate care. They clearly discourage people from accessing care even when the care is needed and even when that care may prevent the need for more expensive treatment later.

For a wealthy individual, a co-pay of hundreds of dollars might be mere "pocket change" and have no impact, while a $3 co-pay can prevent a low-income person from picking up needed medication. When a poor person with an empty stomach has a choice of spending their last dollars on food to ease their hunger or a prescription to address their future mental health needs, most people would opt for the urgent need.

Research bears this out: "Increased cost sharing is associated with lower rates of drug treatment, worse adherence among existing users, and more frequent discontinuation of therapy...For some chronic conditions, higher cost sharing is associated with increased use of medical services, at least for patients with congestive heart failure, lipid disorders, diabetes, and schizophrenia."[128] In

---

128 D. P. Goldman, G. F. Joyce, and Y. Zheng, "Prescription Drug Cost Sharing: Associations with Medication and Medical Utilization and Spending and Health," Journal of the American Medical Association 298:1 (July 4, 2007), pp. 61-69, http://www.ncbi.nlm.nih.gov/pubmed/17609491.

other words, the co-pays and deductibles mean patients are less likely to adhere to their drug therapy, and consequently, more likely to need costly medical services as a result.

No doubt, there are people who overuse health care. But in the United States, the bigger problem is that people under-use health care: they don't get the care they need, when they should. According to the Commonwealth Fund, in 2012, 43% of Americans did not get the care they needed because of cost.[129] Co-pays and deductibles do not lead to more appropriate use of care; to the contrary, they prevented 2 out of every 5 Americans from getting the care they needed.

In Minnesota, more than a quarter of all adults between ages 18 and 64—roughly 900,000 people—did not get medical care due to costs during the past year. Thirty-seven percent of that group said they did not even seek care because they could not afford it.[130]

While the MHP's elimination of co-pays would result in more people getting more care, that doesn't mean treating those patients will cost more. If those visits are medically appropriate, sometimes this will actually reduce costs.

Overall, providing more care to more people costs more, but as pointed out previously, economic analyses and empirical evidence from around the world show that the savings of a universal health care system in other areas are more than enough to pay for that additional care.

There are effective ways of preventing the overuse of health care. The MHP incorporates those practices (See the section, "Preventing the Overuse of Health Care").

---

129 Sara R. Collins, Ruth Robertson, Tracy Garber, and Michelle M. Doty, "Insuring the Future: Current Trends in Health Coverage and the Effects of Implementing the Affordable Care Act," The Commonwealth Fund, April 2013, Exhibit ES-3, http://www.commonwealthfund.org/~/media/files/publications/fund-report/2013/apr/1681_collins_insuring_future_biennial_survey_2012_final.pdf.
130 Minnesota Department of Health, "Minnesota's Adult Uninsured Rate Falls to Lowest Level Yet," December 17, 2014, http://www.health.state.mn.us/news/pressrel/2014/uninsured121714.html.

The MHP would provide early intervention and treatment. The impact of this cannot be overstated. For people suffering with mental illness, this can avoid the need for costly hospitalization, or in some cases, costly incarceration. For people needing dental care, routine visits can prevent life-threatening infections and costly emergency room visits.

Timely, appropriate care is important for optimal health, whether it saves money or costs more. Unfortunately, our current system is so flawed that even cost-saving services are not properly covered. An intensive prevention program in Duluth for people who were recovering from heart failure cut re-hospitalization rates by 82% and lowered the overall, net cost of care for these patients by almost half (48%).[131] Yet this money-saving prevention program was actually losing money for the hospitals involved because the intensive intervention was not reimbursed by health plans.

Our health care system is broken. In the Minnesota Health Plan, lifesaving preventive services like this would be funded statewide, saving lives and in some cases, saving money too—48% savings is real money!

Changes in Upfront & Long-Term Utilization

There would be an initial increase in utilization of medical care when it is available to people who are currently uninsured or underinsured. However, there would also be an immediate reduction in other costly care such as hospitalization for mental illness and use of emergency rooms for routine care, and preventable conditions. Over time, there would be a sustained increase in routine and preventive care, but also sustained and significant decreases in both inappropriate utilization

---

131 Testimony of Linda Wick (Heart Failure Program, St. Mary's Duluth Clinic) before legislative Health Care Access Commission, June 13, 2007.

of care and care that is no longer needed because of primary, secondary, and tertiary preventive care.

Reducing Costs Through Patient/Doctor Decision-Making

Several years ago, the Minnesota Health Care Access Commission heard testimony about how leaving care decisions to patients and doctors does not necessarily lead to more expensive care—as is usually assumed—but frequently leads to decisions not to undergo treatment or to use less expensive alternatives. For example, many patients choose not to have back surgery when a doctor or nurse takes time to explain how less-invasive alternative treatments may have equally good results. Under our current health care system, providers are not always compensated for talking with patients; they are compensated for doing things to patients.

The MHP respects patient choices, including those related to end-of-life treatment. Patients deserve the chance to thoroughly discuss options for their care and provide an advance directive for times when they may be unable to make care decisions.[132]

Giving patients decision-making power for the care they want, and following their directives, avoids costly treatments that patients don't want.

These savings are not mere speculation. The Gundersen Health System in La Crosse, Wisconsin, has received national recognition for its "Respecting Choices" program which gives patients more control over the care they want. Rather than being more expensive, they have documented significant savings by discussing options with patients and letting the patients decide.[133]

---

132   www.tinyurl.com/mhp-2016-bill, p. 19.23.
133   Warren Wolfe, "Preparing for Life's Final Stage," *Star Tribune*, September 22, 2011, http://www.startribune.com/preparing-for-life-s-final-stage/130032813.

F. Beneficial Social and Public Health Impacts

Reduced Welfare and Crime Costs

Under the MHP, the cost savings from some prevention and early intervention investments would not be limited to health care; it would reduce other costs as well. Family planning services for low-income women have been shown to reduce both Medicaid costs and public welfare costs by preventing unintended pregnancies.

These savings are significant. A California study showed better than a 400% return on investment—$4.48 in reduced public expenditures for every dollar spent on family planning.[134]

Chemical Dependency (CD) and Mental Health treatment provides another example. Over 70% of inmates are chemically dependent or substance abusers.[135] Well over half of state prisoners have mental health problems.[136] Giving all Minnesotans access to comprehensive chemical dependency treatment and mental health care would greatly reduce crime and prison costs.

The issue of addiction and chemical dependency deserves special mention. Our current health care system is grossly inadequate when it comes to providing care for people with chemical health problems. Unfortunately, this aspect of care is often ignored when discussing health care reform.

As many as 368,000 Minnesotans struggle with substance

---

134 Rachel Benson Gold, "California Program Shows Benefits of Expanding Family Planning Eligibility," *The Guttmacher Report on Public Policy* 3:5 (October 2000), http://www.guttmacher.org/pubs/tgr/03/5/gr030501.html.
135 Jennifer C. Karberg and Doris J. James, "Substance Dependence, Abuse, and Treatment of Jail Inmates, 2002," *Bureau of Justice Statistics*, July 2005, http://www.bjs.gov/content/pub/pdf/sdatji02.pdf.
136 "Study Finds More Than Half of All Prison and Jail Inmates Have Mental Health Problems," *Bureau of Justice Statistics*, September 6, 2006, http://www.bjs.gov/content/pub/press/mhppjipr.cfm.

abuse.[137] Unfortunately, even when a patient is willing to seek treatment or is forced into it by family, an employer, or the courts, there is often inadequate insurance coverage, or no coverage at all. On top of this, many of those who need treatment are least able to pay for it. Consequently, after an often difficult struggle to get someone to go to treatment, the lack of coverage means the person fails to get the help they need.

When there is coverage, it is often too limited. A person with a severe addiction who might need six months of inpatient treatment, may find their insurance covers only a couple of weeks. Whether there is no coverage or inadequate coverage, the result is that many very sick people are left to cope on their own. Untreated chemical abuse and addiction often leads to lives spiraling out of control, with people losing their jobs, housing, and even their families.

By making comprehensive health care available to all Minnesotans, those who abuse or are addicted to alcohol or other drugs would have much greater access to treatment under the MHP. Because the MHP is responsible for ensuring adequate providers to meet the health care needs, the shortage of chemical dependency treatment programs would be addressed as well.

The consequences of untreated chemical dependency are serious not only for the patient needing treatment, but also for the family and the community. For instance, almost

---

137   "In 2014, about 21.5 million Americans ages 12 and older (8.1%) were classified with a substance use disorder in the past year. Of those, 2.6 million had problems with both alcohol and drugs, 4.5 million had problems with drugs but not alcohol, and 14.4 million had problems with alcohol only." See Substance Abuse and Mental Health Services Administration (SAMHSA), "Mental and Substance Use Disorders," http://www.samhsa.gov/disorders. If Minnesota has the same incidence of substance abuse as the rest of the nation, there would be almost 368,000 Minnesotans with substance use disorders.

a third of children in costly foster care and out-of-home placement are there due to parental alcohol or drug use.[138]

While chemical dependency treatment is expensive, there are numerous studies showing even greater savings as a result. By reducing the use of costly detox and emergency rooms, and by helping preserve families and reduce costly out-of-home placements for children, the savings can be huge. A 1993 CalData study showed that the money spent on chemical dependency treatment had better than a 700% rate of return. It saved taxpayers $7 in reduced crime, health care, and human service costs for each dollar spent, just within the first year of treatment.[139] When counting the benefits to both the public *and* private sectors, savings grow to about $12 for every dollar spent.[140]

In addition to the huge financial savings, there are other benefits to treating chemical dependency, including reduced crime and decreased incidence of child abuse and neglect. Providing comprehensive health care to all not only keeps people healthier but it also decreases crime and keeps people safer.

Return on Investment of Public Health

Several years ago, when the Minnesota Health Care Access Commission was active, the commission had a working group focused on public health. The group recognized the

138 For almost 31 percent of all children placed in foster care in 2012, parental alcohol or drug use was the documented reason for removal. Child Welfare Information Gateway, "Parental Substance Use and the Child Welfare System," *U.S. Department of Health and Human Services, Children's Bureau*, October 2014, p. 2, https://www.childwelfare.gov/pubPDFs/parentalsubabuse.pdf.
139 Neil Swan, "California Study Finds $1 Spent on Treatment Saves Taxpayers $7," *NIDA (National Institute on Drug Abuse) Notes* 10:2 (March/April 1995), http://tinyurl.com/CalDataStudy.
140 National Institute on Drug Abuse, NIH, "Principles of Drug Addiction Treatment," 3rd edition, December 2012, p. 13, http://d14rmgtrwzf5a.cloudfront.net/sites/default/files/podat_1.pdf.

value of public health, and proposed that the state increase public health spending. The resulting Statewide Health Improvement Program (SHIP) invested about $47 million during the first two years, less than $5 per person per year, for grants to communities around the state.

Although the SHIP public health initiative has apparently had success in addressing obesity and reducing the number of people who smoke, funding for it was insignificant in terms of overall health spending. Unfortunately, even that amount has been significantly scaled back since that time, due to a lack of funding from the legislature.

Even at its initial higher level of funding, the SHIP program invested far less than 1/10 of one percent of our total health care expenditures on prevention. When some public health prevention efforts can result in three- or five-fold savings or more, it is financially smart to invest significantly more than that.

Cost savings from public health prevention programs are not limited to medical costs; there are other savings as well.

For example, programs where nurses make home visits to pregnant women and new mothers have been shown to improve pregnancy outcomes as well as reduce child abuse and neglect, decrease criminal behavior, increase maternal employment, and reduce welfare dependency.[141] A study in California has shown these visits have a better than 4 to 1 return on investment.[142]

---

141 D. L. Olds, et al., "Long-Term Effects of Home Visitation on Maternal Life Course and Child Abuse and Neglect: A 15-Year Follow-Up of a Randomized Trial," *Journal of the American Medical Association*, 278:8 (August 27, 1997), pp. 637-643, http://www.ncbi.nlm.nih.gov/pubmed/9272895. See also Nurse-Family Partnership, "Changes in the Mother's Life Course," http://www.nursefamilypartnership.org/proven-results/Changes-in-mother-s-life-course.
142 Ted R. Miller, "Societal Return on Investment in Nurse-Family Partnership Services in California," *Pacific Institute for Research & Evaluation*, http://www.nursefamilypartnership.org/assets/PDF/Communities/CA-Documents/ROI-California.

G. Reduction of Fraud

The MHP would virtually end the fraud (or error) of billing multiple payers for the same service because there would only be one payer. In addition, the more complex a billing and payment system is, the greater the chance for every type of fraud and error. A simple, straightforward system with one payer reduces fraud and error, and makes such problems easier to detect and correct.

H. Reduced Malpractice Insurance Costs

Medical malpractice costs would be sharply reduced under the MHP because the medical expenses arising from a malpractice incident would already be covered by the plan—a significant portion of malpractice awards are used to pay current and future medical costs.[143] In addition, there would be fewer lawsuits, because there would be no need for patients to sue in order to cover medical costs.

On top of the savings from removing medical expenses from malpractice costs, and the reduction in lawsuits, the MHP would likely self-insure doctors for malpractice,[144] reducing costs by eliminating insurance company expenses, underwriting, and profits.

In Canada, physicians are self-insured by the Canadian Medical Protective Association[145] and typically pay premiums that are a fraction of what U.S. physicians pay.[146]

---

143   Herbert M. Kritzer, Guangya Liu, and Neil Vidmar, "An Exploration of 'Noneconomic' Damages in Civil Jury Awards," *William and Mary Law Review* 55 (2014), pp. 971-1027, http://scholarship.law.duke.edu/cgi/viewcontent.cgi?article=5815&context=faculty_scholarship. See p. 993 for a study of jury awards in civil suits in Cook County, IL, which found approximately 21% of damages in medical malpractice cases were devoted to medical costs.
144   tinyurl.com/MHP-2016-bill, p. 18.1.
145   Canadian Medical Protective Association (CMPA), www.cmpa-acpm.ca/about.
146   An illustration comparing malpractice rates between Canada and Florida: "For neurosurgeons in Miami, the annual cost of medical malpractice insurance is astronomical — $237,000, far more than the

One more factor that may reduce malpractice costs: advocates of tort liability limits argue that juries award large settlements because they don't like insurance companies and see those settlements as a way to punish them.[147] If so, by having the MHP be the malpractice insurance carrier, juries would not be going after insurance companies. Juries would see that large settlements would simply increase their costs for the MHP.

Finally, because the Minnesota Health Plan allows patients to choose their doctors, there will be better continuity of care and more trust between patient and doctor, making lawsuits even less likely.

I. Savings in Workers' Compensation and Auto Insurance

The MHP would cover medical expenses arising from workers' compensation and auto accidents, leading to a significant decrease in both workers' compensation and auto insurance costs.

Employers would still be required to have workers' compensation coverage to cover lost wages and pain and suffering, but they would no longer need to pay for costly medical care and rehabilitation, which is *more than half* of the total benefits paid.[148] Likewise drivers would still need auto insurance to cover property damage and liability, but not insurance costs for medical expenses.[149]

---

median price of a house. In Toronto, a neurosurgeon pays about $29,200 for coverage. It's even less in Montreal ($20,600) and Vancouver ($10,650)." see Susan Taylor Martin, "Canada Keeps Malpractice Cost in Check," *Tampa Bay Tribune*, July 26, 2009, http://www.tampabay.com/news/canada-keeps-malpractice-cost-in-check/1021977.

147 Mark Ruquet, "Survey: Insurers Face Bias Among Potential Jurors," *Property Casualty 360*, January 11, 2013, http://www.propertycasualty360.com/2013/01/11/survey-insurers-face-bias-among-potential-jurors.

148 53.9% of benefits paid are for medical and rehabilitation costs. See Minnesota Department of Administration, "2013 Annual Report for State of Minnesota Workers' Compensation Program," April 2014, p. 14, http://archive.leg.state.mn.us/docs/2014/other/140677.pdf.

149 A study of jury awards in civil suits in Cook County, IL, found

This would significantly reduce the lawsuits related to workers compensation and auto insurance. There would be no more legal fights over whether responsibility for medical expenses should be paid by the health plan or the auto insurance or workers compensation plan. Patients seeking treatment for back pain are routinely asked whether their injury came at work or in a car accident. Disputes over who is responsible for medical expenses are a significant additional cost to the system, and that expense does nothing to provide care.

Also, lawyers who handle such cases say that many of their clients had no desire to go to court, but had no other option because the auto insurance or workers comp insurance company cut off their medical treatment before they had received the needed care. This problem would also be eliminated when people get the care they need under the MHP.

J. Employment

Training and Support for Displaced Workers

Regrettably, as with any economic change, the transition to a universal health care system would eliminate jobs of people working for health insurance companies and claims processing for medical providers. It is important not to underestimate the difficulty and challenges faced by people who lose their jobs, regardless of the reason.

Recognizing the moral obligation to assist those facing job transitions as a result of the change, the Minnesota Health Plan would provide retraining and other dislocated worker benefits to quickly move them into new positions.[150]

---

approximately 44% of damages in auto insurance claims were devoted to medical costs. See Herbert M. Kritzer, Guangya Liu, and Neil Vidmar, "An Exploration of 'Noneconomic' Damages in Civil Jury Awards," *William and Mary Law Review* 55 (2014), p. 993, http://scholarship.law.duke.edu/cgi/viewcontent.cgi?article=5815&context=faculty_scholarship.
150   tinyurl.com/MHP-2016-bill, p. 15.11. This is a large, but still

The number of administrative workers in the health sector has grown exponentially in recent decades. With the simple administrative system in the MHP, many of those jobs would no longer be needed. An economic impact analysis of a generic single payer health system in Minnesota estimated that almost 42,800 workers would be displaced.[151] The reality that the MHP eliminates huge administrative costs and hassles is a wonderful benefit in every way except for the fact that we no longer need people to perform many of those administrative functions.

This large displacement of workers is one of the biggest political challenges in adopting a universal health care system to replace our insurance system. However, to put the scope of this job loss in perspective, there are currently about 155,000 Minnesotans leaving their jobs every month,[152] 3½ times as many people as would be

---

manageable cost. Economist Gerald Friedman estimated that it would cost about 1% of total health care spending to pay for dislocated worker benefits and retraining. See Gerald Friedman, "Funding HR 676: The Expanded and Improved Medicare for All Act—How We Can Afford a National Single-Payer Health Plan," July 31, 2013, p. 2 and footnote 6, http://www.pnhp.org/sites/default/files/Funding%20HR%20676_Friedman_7.31.13_proofed.pdf. Because the MHP would likely save significantly more than that, this is a major, but manageable responsibility.

151   The estimated job displacement from a transition to a universal health system would be 16,724 insurance company employees, 22,160 in doctors' offices and medical clinics, and 3,911 in hospitals, totaling 42,795 people. See John Sheils and Megan Cole, "Cost and Economic Impact Analysis of a Single-Payer Plan in Minnesota," Growth & Justice, March 27, 2012, p. 25, http://www.growthandjustice.org/images/uploads/LEWIN.Final_Report_FINAL_DRAFT.pdf.

152   In 2014, the number of people leaving jobs in Minnesota (job "separations") totaled 1,863,527, an average of 155,294 per month, with slightly more new hires per month, 157,788 (the number of job separations includes people leaving their jobs for any reason, whether for taking a new job, being laid off or fired, retirement, or some other reasons). The 155,294 people leaving jobs in any given month is 3½ times the total number of jobs that would be lost in the switch to the MHP. See 2014 Minnesota Unemployment Insurance Wage Records, Minnesota Department of Employment and Economic Development (DEED). Workers dislocated by the transition to the MHP would have many months before any layoffs would occur and many may find new jobs ahead of time on their own.

displaced through the (one time only) transition to the MHP. In essence, the loss of insurance-related jobs due to administrative simplification is less than 2.5 percent of the total number of Minnesotans leaving jobs in any given year.

One potential retraining option would be to help those administrative workers who are interested transition to medical care positions to help address worker shortages in health care. In fact, some insurance company and health provider administrative employees already have the necessary credentials and training and could return to fill much-needed medical positions.

None of this minimizes the pain and challenges caused by the loss of a job, and no one would choose to lay off a large number of good, hardworking people without a very good reason. However, the health improvement (and the lives saved!) by giving timely access to health care to all Minnesotans, as well as the huge economic savings, are much needed.

In addition to the retraining and dislocated worker benefits that the MHP would provide, it is worth pointing out that these laid-off workers would be fully covered for all of their medical needs, the same as all other Minnesotans under the MHP. Currently, the loss of health coverage is one of the most expensive and dangerous problems laid-off workers face. Not having to worry about getting health care after a layoff is an incredible help.

Enabling Minnesota Employers to Hire More Workers

Fortunately, helping those displaced workers find new positions would be easier because the MHP would create far more jobs than would be lost in the transition.[153] The

153 Several studies showing significant job growth from a transition to single payer are cited by Amy Lange in "Beyond the Affordable Care Act:

big picture is that our current health care system's high costs and limited access inhibits economic growth. A 2010 survey of Minnesota employers found that the expense of health coverage was the most significant obstacle to business expansion.[154] A sizable portion of the price of Minnesota products is driven by the expense of providing health care to employees. By addressing those problems, enactment of the MHP would stimulate the economy and create new jobs. It would free businesses to expand without worrying about finding, negotiating, and paying so much for health care benefits for their employees.

Entrepreneurs, farmers, and other self-employed individuals would be able to work full-time on their business ventures rather than needing to hold another job that has health benefits. The MHP would be a strong jobs magnet, enabling Minnesota businesses to increase hiring and potentially attracting businesses from other states, providing additional new job opportunities for laid-off administrative workers.

An Economic Analysis of a Unified System of Health Care for Minnesota," pp. 27-28, *Growth & Justice*, March 2012, http://growthandjustice.org/publication/BeyondACA.pdf. One estimate nationally projects 2.6 million new permanent jobs from adoption of a national single payer system.
154   Chen May Yee, "Businesses: Health Care Costs Stymie Expansion," *Star Tribune*, February 9, 2010, http://tinyurl.com/HCcostshurtbizgrowth.

6. Health Care for All, No Exceptions

When viewed as a short-term, temporary fix, the federal Affordable Care Act (ACA) does provide health insurance to many who were uninsured. It also prevents insurance companies from dumping sick people and allows many young people to be covered under their parents' policies. The ACA is making a life-saving difference for many.

However, even though the ACA has expanded coverage, almost 5% of Minnesotans (about 264,500 people)[155] remain uninsured. There are a number of other barriers to care post-ACA as well. Many among the 95% who have insurance still cannot access needed medical care because of high deductibles, co-pays, gaps in their coverage, and limited networks.

The reality is that people will continue to fall through the cracks of our health care system until all people are covered for all the care they need, until people can visit the health care provider of their choice, and until we have a progressive way for people to pay for coverage.

The bottom line is that we still have much work to do to on health care reform post-ACA. The Minnesota Health Plan would provide health *care*, not health *insurance*, to every Minnesotan, with no exceptions.

A. Health Care for All is a Moral Issue

We make the *medical* case for the Minnesota Health Plan because of its ability to improve both public health and the health of individuals through the logical, efficient delivery of health care to all.

---

155 For data as of May 2014, see State Health Access Data Assistance Center (SHADAC), "Early Impacts of the Affordable Care Act on Health Insurance Coverage in Minnesota," June 2014, http://shadac.org/ MinnesotaCoverageReport.

We also make the *economic* case, about how covering all people, for all of their medical needs, is less expensive than our current, convoluted insurance system.

But this is, fundamentally, a *moral* issue. It is a matter of justice, a matter of compassion, a matter of fairness. We cannot ignore the cruelty of avoidable pain and suffering caused by the failure to cover dental care. We cannot consider it acceptable that people do not have a doctor check out a potentially life-threatening condition because they cannot afford to pay the deductible. We cannot fail to recognize the lives we destroy by denying treatment to young adults struggling with mental health crises.

> *"Of all the forms of inequality, injustice in health care is the most shocking and inhumane."*
>
> — Dr. Martin Luther King, Jr.

Health statistics show Minnesota does better than other states. But those statistics show that there are huge gaps in our health system in Minnesota. And behind those statistics are real people and real lives.

Our health care system is not acceptable, and will never be acceptable, as long as it causes people to go bankrupt over medical bills and as long as it blocks people from getting needed care, causing unnecessary suffering, or even death. Dr. Martin Luther King said that, "Of all the forms of inequality, injustice in health care is the most shocking and inhumane."[156]

The Affordable Care Act increased the number of people with health insurance so more people have access to some care. But the ACA, and proposed modifications to the ACA, fail to cover everyone for all their medical needs.

---

156 Dr. Martin Luther King, Jr., March 25, 1966, speech to the Medical Committee for Human Rights.

Minnesota has some of the world's best medical professionals, health facilities, medical research, and technology. We have a moral responsibility to develop a health system to match.

When other nations are able cover all of their people for all of their needs, there is no excuse for our failure to do so.

B. Truly Universal: Why Health *Care* Instead of Health *Insurance*

Some believe that if we simply expand the Affordable Care Act, we could eventually get "universal" coverage. Unfortunately, universal insurance coverage alone is not sufficient—it does not guarantee access to care. You must also have:

- **seamless coverage**, so people are covered continuously throughout their lives, without gaps in coverage due to loss of employment or change in income or family;

- **comprehensive benefits**, so all medical needs are covered;

- **a progressive payment structure**, so all pay for health care, but at varying levels that are affordable for all; and

- **patient choice**, so that patients can choose to get care from providers they trust, and that appropriate medical decisions are made by health care providers, not insurance companies.

The MHP provides coverage from birth until death, regardless of health, financial, or employment status. Coverage follows you if you travel, retire, or lose your job. This matters in overall public health, and it is essential in order to address health disparities.

Health Insurance System Leaves Deadly Gaps

To understand the failure of the health insurance system, let's turn to a front page feature story in the Minneapolis Star Tribune back in July 2011. The article profiled a Minnesota family that had health insurance, but could not get needed mental health treatment for their son. The story contained excerpts from a long interview with the mother talking about the family's extensive, but largely unsuccessful efforts to get the care her son needed.

Kathy Swanson described how her son was severely challenged even at age 3, when he took a knife and slashed the upholstery of the kitchen chairs. She told how they were forced to hide even the kitchen knives from their pre-school son. The story documented all of the parents' efforts, throughout their son's childhood, to get him appropriate treatment.

One summer early in his teenage years, the article described how after a hospitalization of their son, they finally got him into a 30-day treatment plan at a residential program for youth with serious mental illness. "But Swanson was forced to leave after 13 days, after spraying a counselor with a fire extinguisher. His mother was shocked. The facility had secure rooms for deviant kids, and counselors had told her that misbehaviors were breakthrough opportunities to connect with kids.

"She suspects that another factor was behind her son's early release: Her health insurance had a cap of 10 days of residential care, and the home had just learned of this," according to the paper.

Another time, the son's social worker tried to get him admitted to another residential treatment center. But he wasn't admitted because they didn't have a court order requiring placement "and her health insurance wouldn't cover the cost," according to the article.

Most readers of the article likely felt great sympathy for the Swanson family over their problems. Still, under our health care system, we think of it as their problem, not ours.

It is their problem, until you recognize that the reason the article was featured on the front page of the Sunday paper was that their son is the young man who stole a car and some guns and killed two convenience store clerks in Iowa.[157]

The unmet health care needs of that young man didn't just affect his family, it affected all of us. It is of little comfort to the many victims of this tragedy that the young man, now in prison, is finally getting the mental health treatment he needed all along.

In this case, as in too many others, health insurance is a barrier to getting the health care people need. It is not that insurance is inherently good or bad, it is that few health insurance policies in Minnesota cover all necessary care, and most have inappropriate caps on the amount of treatment covered because of the (short term) economic interests of the health plans. Even if coverage would, over time, save money, insurance plans do not benefit from long term savings, because they do not end up paying the long term costs. It is only through a universal health plan with long-term societal responsibility in mind—cradle to grave—that the plan is able to cover all health care needs because it is in the social and economic interest over one's lifetime.

We need a health care system that provides care when it is needed, not a health insurance system that pays for treating some of the needs of those who have the right insurance plan.

---

157 Jeremy Olson, "Did the System Fail a Budding Killer?" *Star Tribune*, July 17, 2011. http://www.startribune.com/did-system-fail-a-budding-killer/125693298/

C. Creating a System without Cracks in Coverage

Whenever there are gaps, or cracks, in health care coverage, people fall through those cracks. Even though there are multiple methods through which people can obtain health insurance—through family, employment, COBRA, public or private coverage in the health insurance exchange, private insurance outside of the exchange, or Medicare and other public programs—there are transitions where gaps can and will occur. And there are gaps in most of that coverage even for those who are covered.

For example, people whose coverage through work is lost when they are laid off may be able to buy coverage through COBRA if they can afford it, or perhaps through the insurance exchange. However, dealing with the stress of a layoff, and the loss of income from it, means that some laid off workers may not promptly get replacement coverage.

Or, a person whose coverage comes through a spouse may be left without coverage after a divorce. Again, in an ideal situation, the newly uninsured person might immediately get replacement coverage, but the stress from a divorce along with greater financial challenges means that some will, at least temporarily, fall through the cracks.

Many people who have serious mental health, addiction, or other chronic health conditions, are struggling just to survive, and getting health insurance is not always on their agenda, even though they are the ones most in need of health care.

On top of that, those who most need health care are often the people who have the worst coverage. Dental care is, for many who need it, a separate, expensive insurance plan that is not included in their health insurance.

These multiple gaps in access to health coverage cause, or aggravate, many health disparities. The only way to stop people from falling through the cracks is to eliminate those cracks and make health care available to all, as the Minnesota Health Plan would.

Recent immigrants, people with low incomes, and those who are laid off or in job transitions would all be fully covered by the MHP. Homeless people and those struggling with mental illness or addiction will no longer need to turn to emergency rooms, detox, or jail for their medical care. By serving all people, and providing culturally-specific care and interpretive services, the MHP will significantly improve public health.

Under the MHP, every Minnesotan will have the same high quality health care that wealthy CEOs and elected public officials receive. That is a big step forward in addressing health disparities.

D. Covering All Medical Needs

Even if we were able to cover every Minnesotan with a health plan through a combination of MNsure, employer sponsored plans, individual policies, and all other sources, that still would not be sufficient to give everyone access to medical care. To ensure everyone has the medical care they need, those health plans would need to have comprehensive benefits.

Currently, some families have to deal with multiple insurance companies to get care. Not only do they have different insurance companies for different family members (due to employment, disability, or age), but most need separate insurance plans for dental care. Those with "Long Term Care" coverage for nursing home expenses have a separate insurance plan for that. And seniors on Medicare, who now have "prescription drug coverage," have a separate insurance plan for that as well.

Oral health is an example of how our current system picks winners and losers by providing only incomplete health care benefits. In addition to dramatically impacting quality of life, oral health is a factor in major medical conditions such as heart disease, diabetes, and adverse pregnancy outcomes.[158] While the ACA acknowledged the importance of dental coverage by requiring that plans for children offer dental coverage as an option, parents are not required to purchase it for their children and there is no dental coverage requirement for adults.[159] This lack of dental coverage is pennywise and pound foolish—by failing to cover dental care, we lose the opportunity to identify and treat preventable diseases before they get out of control and become extremely expensive.

E. Long-Term Care

Long-term care is an integral part of health care. If a plan is truly going to address all health care needs, it must include coverage for long-term care (LTC). Like dental, mental health, and other aspects of care that are often excluded from health insurance coverage, LTC would also be covered by MHP.

For people who live to age 65, "more than two-thirds will need assistance to deal with a loss in functioning at some point during their remaining years of life."[160] In other words, they will need long-term care. About 80% of them will receive that care in the community,[161] not in nursing homes, but they will need care.

---

158 National Institute of Dental and Craniofacial Research, "Surgeon General's Report on Oral Health," part 3, last updated March 7, 2014, http://www.nidcr.nih.gov/DataStatistics/SurgeonGeneral/sgr/part3.htm.

159 HealthCare.gov, "Dental Coverage in the Marketplace," https://www.healthcare.gov/coverage/dental-coverage.

160 Congressional Budget Office, "Rising Demand for Long-Term Services and Supports for Elderly People," June 2013, https://www.cbo.gov/sites/default/files/113th-congress-2013-2014/reports/44363-LTC.pdf.

161 Ibid.

The average cost of long-term care in Minnesota is $57,000 per year—almost the same as the $59,000 median household income in the state.[162] However, because of the high expense of such care, it is often treated as a separate entity, similar to dental care. In Minnesota, long-term care (including home health care services) is about 15% of total health care spending.[163]

Current Financing System is Broken

Although long-term care is needed by a large number of older adults and people with disabilities, and it is not affordable to most, it is not covered by health insurance or Medicare (except for brief periods after some hospitalizations). Many people are surprised to learn that Medicare does not cover most nursing home care and long-term home care.

To fill this gap, the state and federal government have tried to encourage people to purchase long-term care (LTC) insurance on their own, providing tax credits and other incentives. However, despite significant efforts, relatively few people purchase such coverage.

Families are overwhelmed by the high cost of that coverage, the complexity of figuring out what kind of LTC insurance is needed, and which exclusions in the policies might make them inadequate for one's needs.

On top of this, buying long-term care when you are young and healthy does not guarantee low premiums forever. A couple years ago, some Minnesotans saw almost a doubling of premiums in a single year.[164]

---

162 Correspondence from Loren Colman (Assistant Commissioner of Minnesota Department of Human Services), April 6, 2016.

163 Minnesota Department of Health, "Minnesota Health Care Spending and Projections, 2012," June 2014, Table 3, http://www.health.state.mn.us/divs/hpsc/hep/publications/costs/healthspending2014.pdf.

164 "Premiums are soaring by 20 to 90 percent for thousands of Minnesotans who carry long-term care insurance, and many older people

William Baldwin, a former Forbes Magazine editor, described the problem this causes:

"The LTC policy permits the seller to change the terms after you have put money in. LTC policyholders have confronted surprise rate hikes on the order of 45% to 85%. They then have the unpleasant choice of either walking away from the premiums they have sunk so far or else throwing good money after bad.

"Imagine buying a Lexus for $5,000 down plus $500 a month under a contract that allows the dealer to raise the monthly payment if he wants to. Six months in, it goes to $800, and you have a free choice between paying up or handing in the car and losing your down payment. That would be a ridiculous contract to sign. LTC buyers sign contracts like that."[165]

Purchasing LTC insurance early, as financial advisors and government agencies recommend, doesn't do any good if rates jump at a later date to a point that the policyholder can no longer afford the premiums and they lose the coverage after investing large amounts earlier.

"It's a bit murky just when a policyholder is sufficiently disabled to be entitled to collect. If a benefit worth $50,000 is at stake, it makes sense for the insurer to spend $45,000 on medical exams and claims adjusters fighting the claim and for the applicant to spend $45,000 pursuing it."[166]

Because of the large expense of such LTC coverage, and

---

are struggling to figure out what to do." Warren Wolfe, "Minnesota Seniors Facing a Spike in Long-term Care Cost," *Star Tribune*, March 19, 2012, http://www.startribune.com/minnesota-seniors-facing-a-spike-in-long-term-care-cost/143267316/.

165   William Baldwin, "Dodge the Long Term Care Insurance Mess," *Forbes*, March 29, 2013.

166   Ibid.

uncertainty of what policies to buy, most Minnesotans who end up in a nursing home or needing intensive home care do not have insurance that covers it.

In the end, Medicaid (known in Minnesota as *Medical Assistance*) does step in when someone needs long-term care but has no money to pay the bills. However, Medicaid does not pay the bills until the family has lost virtually all of their savings and assets.

To prevent the loss of all assets, some elderly couples have felt they had no option but to get a divorce. Not because they want one, but because it is the only way they have to keep the healthy spouse from going into poverty.

Others, to avoid losing all of their savings, give their savings to children and grandchildren prematurely, to shield those assets from nursing home costs. This leads to the state reaching back several years from when a parent goes into a nursing home, in an attempt to recapture those assets.

Like the rest of the health care system, **our system for financing long-term care is broken**. Most people are not adequately covered for LTC and there is significant financial maneuvering to hide assets (by patients) or capture them (by Medicaid).

Covering Long-Term Care under the MHP

The same reasons for covering all Minnesotans for all their other medical needs apply to long-term care as well. Minnesota already recognizes the importance of coverage for long-term care, and covers a major portion of it through Medical Assistance. In fact, when you count Medical Assistance and other programs, government funds are already paying about three-fourths of the costs of long-term care in Minnesota.[167]

---

167 Health Economics Program, Minnesota Department of Health,

In other words, all of the agony over long-term care costs and LTC insurance and all of the other problems related to access to care is being fought over just the remaining one-fourth of long-term care costs that are not already paid for by taxpayers.

By covering all Minnesotans, the system would be fair to all, and we would eliminate the dysfunctional payment system we currently have.

That is important, because while long-term care is expensive, Minnesota families and businesses end up paying not just for the care, but also for the administrative waste. By ending the costly, time-consuming struggles families face in getting and retaining LTC insurance, *and* getting the plan to pay claims, *and* ending the costly and time consuming efforts to shelter assets from Medicaid, *and* eliminating the need for the state to recover those assets, *and* ending administrative hassles over collecting from multiple payers who are attempting to shift the costs to others, Minnesota would likely be able to deliver the same amount of long-term care for less cost.

However, by including LTC coverage, there is an additional complication in converting from the current funding system to universal long-term care coverage. If all costs of a nursing home are covered, it could create a financial incentive for people to place a family member into a facility before such a move is needed, in order to save on housing, food, and other living expenses.

As a result, the MHP board would be authorized to charge people for the room and board costs.[168] For low income people who meet the Medicaid income limits, those expenses would be covered, as they are now.

---

personal communication, 2015.
168 tinyurl.com/MHP-2016-bill, p. 6.4.

The bottom line is that long-term care is an important aspect of health care, and it needs to be included in a comprehensive health care system. By covering it for all Minnesotans, Minnesota families and businesses will end up paying significantly less for it than they do now.

F. Addressing Health Disparities

In recent years, Minnesota has begun to recognize the serious problem of health disparities. The Minnesota Department of Health issued an excellent report, *Advancing Health Equity in Minnesota,* early in 2014. That report goes far beyond what other states have done in acknowledging health disparities and spelling out changes that must be made. A cover letter signed by all of Governor Dayton's agency heads described the issue clearly:

> "Stark inequalities persist in some parts of our society, and these inequalities have resulted in some groups having better health outcomes than others—even after factoring in individual choices. For Minnesota to have the brightest future possible we need to eliminate these health disparities, especially those experienced by people of color and American Indians.

> "Health is created by much more than just good medical care. Optimal health for everyone requires excellent schools, economic opportunities, environmental quality, secure housing, good transportation, safe neighborhoods, and much more."[169]

Health Commissioner Ed Ehlinger pointed out that while Minnesotans are, on average, "among the healthiest in the country," the disparities here are among the worst.

---

169 Minnesota Department of Health, "Advancing Health Equity in Minnesota: Report to the Legislature," February 1, 2014, http://www.health. state.mn.us/divs/chs/healthequity/ahe_leg_report_020414.pdf.

The Health Department report[170] quantified some of the impacts in Minnesota:

- African American and American Indian babies die in the first year of life at twice the rate of white babies.

- American Indian, Hispanic/Latino, and African American youth have the highest rates of obesity.

- Intimate partner violence affects 11 to 24 percent of high school seniors, with the highest rates among American Indian, African American, and Hispanic/Latino students.

- African American and Hispanic/Latino women in Minnesota are more likely to be diagnosed with later-stage breast cancer.

- Gay, lesbian, and bisexual university students are more likely than their heterosexual peers to struggle with their mental health.

- Persons with serious and persistent mental illness die, on average, 25 years earlier than the general public.

The *Advancing Health Equity in Minnesota*[171] report also documents some of the social and economic disparities that contribute to these health disparities:

- Poverty rates for children under 18 in Minnesota are twice as high for Asian children, three times as high for Hispanic/Latino children, four times as high for American Indian children, and nearly five times as high for African American children as for white children.

- Unemployment is highest among populations of color, American Indians, and people who live in rural Minnesota.

---

170 Ibid.
171 Ibid.

- While 75 percent of the white population in Minnesota owns their own home, only 21 percent of African Americans, 45 percent of Hispanic/Latinos, 47 percent of American Indians, and 54 percent of Asian Pacific Islanders own their own homes.

- African Americans and Hispanic/Latinos in Minnesota have less than half the per-capita income of the white population.

- Lesbian, gay, bisexual, and transgender youth are at increased risk for bullying, teasing, harassment, physical assault, and suicide-related behaviors compared to other students.

- Low-income students are more likely to experience residential instability, as indicated by the frequency of changing schools, than their higher-income peers in every racial and ethnic category.

- American Indian, Hispanic/Latino, and African American youth have the lowest rates of on-time high school graduation.

- African Americans and American Indians are incarcerated at nine times the rate of white persons.

Dr. Ehlinger summarized, "We know that health is determined not just by access to high quality health care but also by healthy social, economic, and environmental conditions... We also know that it will take a commitment from all parts of our society, not just those in the health care and public health fields, to achieve this public health goal of health equity." Dr. Ehlinger expressed his hope that we "are at a landmark moment when *eliminating health disparities and achieving health equity is recognized as a necessity for the overall long-term welfare of our state.*"[172]

---

172 Ibid. Emphasis added.

In other words, we're all in this together—we all benefit
when others in our community are healthy. Eliminating
disparities in health, whether they are caused by poverty,
race, age, employment status, or any other factor, requires
more than replacing our dysfunctional health insurance
system. However, *providing universal access* to health care
through a seamless system, with no cracks in coverage
for people to fall into, *is a necessary condition for ending
disparities.*

By providing comprehensive health care benefits,
extensive, far-reaching public health services, and
breaking down barriers to access—including economic,
language, and transportation barriers—the MHP would
reduce disparities.

It would benefit all Minnesotans, but those who are at the
bottom end of the disparities would benefit most. For low
income people, by helping address their health problems,
it would begin to break the cycle between poverty and
poor health, where poor health prevents people from
working, and the resulting low income increases their
health challenges.

Undocumented Immigrants

One group of people who are currently excluded
from coverage under the Affordable Care Act are
undocumented immigrants. The issue of undocumented
immigrants needs to be addressed by the federal
government with comprehensive immigration reform.

Undocumented immigrants currently living in Minnesota
already receive health care. Unfortunately, we often
provide it at the most expensive stage—in emergency
rooms and hospitalization. Under the MHP, they would
get health care at an earlier, less costly stage.

As a society, we share an interest in ensuring that all
who live in our state are as healthy as possible. When

one segment of the community does not get the health care they need, it puts the rest of the population at risk. For example, if someone is abusing alcohol, the failure to provide treatment puts everyone at greater risk from drunk driving and other alcohol-related crimes, whether that individual is an immigrant or not. If a segment of the population has untreated communicable diseases such as TB, influenza, or sexually-transmitted infections, the rest of the population is at much greater risk of exposure to those diseases.

If the people handling our food in meat packing plants or serving us burgers at McDonald's get infectious diseases, does anyone believe it makes sense to deny them treatment because of their immigration status and let them spread those diseases to everyone else?

G. Preventing Overuse of Health Care

As mentioned earlier, despite multiple efforts to address the overuse of health care by some Americans (most of those efforts being bureaucratic and costly), there are some people and providers who *do* overuse the system. The Minnesota Health Plan would work to reduce overuse of health care by addressing many of the factors driving that use, including:

- facilitating more patient/doctor decision-making and letting patients know their options. This leads to care that informed patients desire—often far less intrusive, less costly care than is given when patients have less information about what is being done to them;

- providing care coordination. This helps patients get the vaccinations and tests they need, while avoiding redundant tests ordered by providers who are unaware that the patients have already had them done;

- reducing costly emergency room use, by giving all people easy access to routine and urgent care. This removes the problem of uninsured people using the ER because it is the only care they know how to access;

- eliminating provider conflicts of interest in referring patients for more tests and procedures;

- eliminating direct-to-consumer marketing of pharmaceuticals, which drives patient demand for inappropriate medications;

- reducing excess capacity of medical facilities and equipment—when there is a medical technology "arms race" between hospitals and clinics, the owners *need* to give expensive treatments to more people to cover the high cost of what would otherwise be underutilized equipment; and

- reducing the need for costly care through public health and prevention—addressing issues like obesity and diabetes through public health saves big money.

Despite spending about twice as much on health care per person than other industrialized nations, this high cost is *not* because Americans are always running to the doctor for unnecessary care. The average American visits the doctor 4 times per year. In contrast, Japanese residents average 12.9 doctor visits; residents of France 6.4 visits; Germans, 9.9; and Norwegians, 4.2 visits.[173] Our costs are driven not by overuse of health care, but by a bloated, administrative system that fails to give appropriate care when it is needed.

---

173 For the most current data, see the section on Doctor Consultations per Capita in "OECD Health Statistics 2014—Frequently Requested Data," http://www.oecd.org/els/health-systems/oecd-health-statistics-2014-frequently-requested-data.htm.

7. Prior Payment Reforms Haven't Worked

A. Prior Reforms *Increased* Administrative Costs

Because of the high cost of health care, many of the health care reforms pursued in Minnesota and the U.S. over the past 40 years have focused on the desire to save money. Unfortunately, those experiments haven't always delivered savings. Even after some widely hyped, "cost-saving" health reform initiatives, our health care costs have risen much faster than inflation.

For example, Health Maintenance Organizations (HMOs) were established beginning in the 1970s with the intent to provide "managed care," which would have incentives to deliver less "unnecessary" treatment,[174] thereby saving money. However, they needed large administrative systems in order to function.[175] As a result, HMOs or Managed Care Organizations (MCOs) needed to deliver huge

---

174 John D. Ehrlichman, in a taped conversation with President Richard Nixon in 1971 that led to the HMO act of 1973, said: "All the incentives are toward less medical care, because the less care they [HMOs] give them, the more money they make." Note that the rationale given by Ehrlichman does not mention reducing *unnecessary* care, but reducing *care* whether necessary or not, in order to save the insurance company money. University of Virginia Check—February 17, 1971, 5:26 pm-5:53 pm, Oval Office Conversation 450-23. Look for: tape rmn_e450c. A transcript of the conversation is available at https://en.wikisource.org/wiki/Transcript_of_ taped_conversation_between_President_Richard_Nixon_and_John_D._ Ehrlichman_(1971)_that_led_to_the_HMO_act_of_1973.

175 "'As managed care enrollment has soared so have administrative expenses,' said Dr. Steffie Woolhandler, Associate Professor of Medicine at Harvard. 'The percentage of workers in the health system dealing with paperwork has increased from 18% to nearly 30%, belying the myth of HMO efficiency.'" See *Physicians for a National Health Program*, "Claim That HMO's Save Money Is Little More Than 'Folklore,' Health Affairs Study Finds," March 2000, http://www.pnhp.org/news/2000/march/claim_that_ hmos_sav.php.

health care savings *just to break even* and cover those high administrative costs. There is no evidence that they did so.

There is one clear result from all of the health care reforms of the last 40 years: a huge growth in health care administrators.

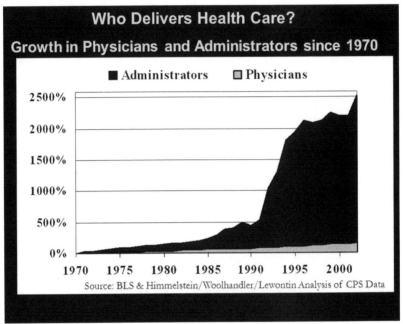

Since 1970, there has been about a tripling in the number of physicians, but the number of health administrators has grown by almost 30-fold.[176]

Minnesota and the nation are currently in the midst of a big new reform experiment, creating Accountable Care Organizations (ACOs) to deliver care. There is one troubling similarity between the ACO experiment now and the HMO experiment in the 1970s: there were no HMOs in existence to demonstrate savings then, and there were no ACOs in 2010 before the ACA was adopted

---

176 Chart from Physicians for a National Health Program, http://www. pnhp.org/PDF_files/PNHPBrochure.pdf.

that could provide empirical evidence that ACOs will save money.

Instead, the push for ACOs was based on the completely reasonable logic that health care providers will deliver care more efficiently if they work together and assume total responsibility for some types of care, because they will make more money if they are efficient, or lose money if they aren't.

However, there is reason for skepticism here because the nation, including Minnesota, is spending billions of dollars implementing ACOs and driving additional growth in health administrative costs before we know whether the experiment will actually reduce treatment costs. The early evidence is not very promising. "After paying bonuses to the strong performers, the ACO program resulted in a net loss of nearly $3 million to the Medicare trust fund," according to the federal government.[177] That loss, while relatively minor, is a loss not a gain, which is not what ACO proponents were hoping for. Furthermore, it does not account for the higher administrative costs faced by hospitals and clinics, which could make the losses (i.e., *higher* health care costs) much more substantial.

Perhaps because of those higher costs faced by providers, many are rethinking their participation in ACOs, and some have dropped out. Ezekiel Emmanuel, in a commentary in the Wall Street Journal in 2015, described the results of the ACO experiment as "less than encouraging," and pointed out how many providers are dropping out of the program.[178]

---

177 Jordan Rau and Jenny Gold, "Medicare Yet To Save Money Through Heralded Medical Payment Model," *Kaiser Health News*, September 14, 2015, http://khn.org/news/medicare-yet-to-save-money-through-heralded-medical-payment-model.
178 Ezekiel Emanuel and Topher Spiro, "The Coming Shock in Health-

Again, not only must ACOs drive medical costs down, they must drive them down enough to recoup all of those increased administrative costs *before* there are any net savings.

In addition to the higher administrative costs required for ACOs, they are disrupting other parts of our current medical system. Small medical practices are often forced to merge with large hospital/healthcare systems in order to implement the risk-sharing payment system that ACOs are designed to deliver.[179]

Forcing small medical clinics to join big provider systems could potentially make medical care better, but it could potentially make it worse, and certainly less personal. To be clear, the point of these mergers under ACOs is not to improve care, but to explore whether they might save money. The risk is that when this experiment is finished, it is possible that these mergers will actually *reduce* the quality of care and cost *more*.

Unfortunately, there is recent evidence that these mergers are driving costs higher. A December 2015 study from Yale University, "The Price Ain't Right? Hospital Prices and Health Spending on the Privately Insured," found that the large hospital/health care systems created by mergers to form Accountable Care Organizations, were actually driving up prices, thus increasing health spending.[180]

Care Cost Increases," *Wall Street Journal*, July 7, 2015, http://www.wsj.com/articles/SB11301772451238044816904581084584272004382.

179   Elizabeth Stawicki, "Independent Medical Practices Find It Harder to Stay that Way," *MPR News*, May 16, 2011, http://www.mprnews.org/story/2011/05/14/independent-medical-practice.

180   Zack Cooper, et al., "The Price Ain't Right? Hospital Prices and Health Spending on the Privately Insured," *Health Care Pricing Project*, December 2015, http://www.healthcarepricingproject.org/sites/default/files/pricing_variation_manuscript_0.pdf. See also Kevin Quealy and Sanger-Katz, Margot, "The Experts Were Wrong About the Best Places for Better

Regardless of the outcome from ACOs, one cannot argue that it was an *evidence-based* reform. Proponents of both the HMO and the ACO concepts were, and are, convinced that their ideas will improve health care and save money, but in both cases they were creative, but untested, ideas.

In contrast, there is evidence that a single health plan (with a single payer) will cut costs. The concept of using a single health plan instead of a multiple payer system has been tried. Based on empirical evidence from health care systems in the US (the Veterans Administration system and Medicare) and from around the world, it *does* save money.

B. Impacts on Quality of Care

Complexity Hurts Quality

The result of these alternative payment models is that medical providers are hiring more people to fill out paperwork and less people to deliver care. The owner of one medical company serving people in assisted living said that he hired over a dozen additional licensed practical nurses (LPNs) in 2015, not to provide care, but to assist in coding and billing—purely paper shuffling—related to new, more complex alternative payment systems.[181]

Spending more on administrative work takes time away from delivering care. These increased administrative costs could only be justified if there is strong evidence that it will improve care or save more than those extra efforts cost.

In addition, there is a growing concern about physician burnout from frustration over rapidly increasing paperwork, as doctors must meet data collection and

and Cheaper Health Care," *New York Times*, December 15, 2015, http://www.nytimes.com/interactive/2015/12/15/upshot/the-best-places-for-better-cheaper-health-care-arent-what-experts-thought.html?_r=4.
181   Personal communication, December 8, 2015.

reporting required by these new payment models. Doctors talk about "filling out forms" and "checking boxes" rather than treating patients. Burnout is a very real cost of these payment reforms.

Rather than setting up complicated new payment structures with the hope that they will provide incentives for better care, we should be spending those resources *directly* on improved care.

Improving Quality

Improving the quality of health care is a top priority for everyone involved in health care policy. When providers do not understand best practices, or fail to implement them appropriately, it can have serious, even deadly consequences (for example, with hospital-acquired infections).

Collecting data, studying outcomes, and conducting research are activities necessary for quality improvement. Then, as medical experts find protocols and treatments that deliver better results, it is important to develop guidelines for best practices and disseminate them to medical providers and to those who work on health and public health policy. Education and continuing education for medical professionals, along with mentoring and peer-to-peer coaching, can help providers know the latest research and work to improve their practices. This is essential for any high quality health care system, and is integrated throughout the Minnesota Health Plan.

Problems with *Pay for Performance, Value-Based Purchasing, & Quality* Payment Reforms

Unfortunately, most "quality"-based payment reforms are far removed from that simple protocol of finding more effective treatments, developing best practices, educating and training medical professionals in them, and encouraging those professionals to work on improving their practice. When our health care system moves beyond evidence-based quality improvement efforts, with well-intentioned reforms that seek to pay for health care based on "quality," there are problems.

Not only are there high administrative costs for grading each individual health care service and designing a payment system to reward quality, but there is also evidence that such payment systems are counterproductive, increase health disparities, and discourage quality care.

Unfortunately, raising concerns about these initiatives is politically challenging because of the marketing terminology used by proponents. "Pay for Performance" or "Value-Based Purchasing" or "Accountable Care" are terms (often used interchangeably) that discourage questioning by making it sound as if anyone who is not enthusiastically supporting such proposals is against value, quality, or accountability.

This is not merely an academic concern. Minnesota and the nation are rapidly moving forward in adopting alternative payment models, despite little evidence of the wisdom of making the changes. Minnesota has a goal of getting 60% of the population in alternative payment models by 2016,[182] despite a lack of evidence that those models actually save money or improve care.

The concept of Value-Based Purchasing sounds promising: we want to pay for high quality care that works, not waste money on treatments that don't work. But in order to do so, one needs to measure the care being delivered. And measuring the success for each of

---

182   See p. 5, showing Minnesota's goal of having 60% of fully insured Minnesotans in an alternative payment model by 2016, presentation of Minnesota Multi-Payer Alignment Task Force, "Minnesota Accountable Health Model," September 16, 2015, tinyurl.com/huzuddz.

thousands of treatments and services is a very complex and costly task.

On top of that, the measurements do not properly account for other factors, such as health and socioeconomic differences in patients, which can have a bigger impact on outcomes than the care received in a clinic. The Minnesota Department of Health says "90 percent of health outcomes are affected by factors outside of clinical care."[183] The costly task of measuring outcomes is only valuable if it is accurate *and* can be accurately adjusted to account for the differences between patients.

Value-Based Purchasing May Increase Disparities

In light of Minnesota's strong desire to reduce health disparities, it is important to recognize that these alternative payment models may actually be making health disparities worse.

The 2015 Minnesota Health Care Financing Task Force received testimony from the Health Care Safety Net Coalition that because quality measures do not adjust for differences in patient populations, clinics that serve communities and people facing socioeconomic challenges receive low "quality" scores even if they provide high quality care.

The coalition used the example: "Quality scores for diabetes care are based in part on whether the patient uses tobacco. If the patient uses tobacco, the clinic fails the entire diabetes quality measure." They pointed out that there is a huge variation in smoking rates between different racial and ethnic groups and that a disproportionate number of low income people smoke. A document distributed by the Safety Net Coalition said

---

183 Minnesota Department of Health, "Advancing Health Equity in Minnesota: Report to the Legislature," February 1, 2014, p. 13, http://www. health.state.mn.us/divs/chs/healthequity/ahe_leg_report_020414.pdf.

that as a result, "a clinic with high clinical quality of care that serves more American Indian and African American patients will receive lower quality scores," which leads to lower payments if their payments are linked to those scores.[184]

Tying payments to those scores harms the clinics "that specialize in providing culturally appropriate care and additional services to overcome socioeconomic barriers. Clinics may be forced to make cuts, reduce services, or close. It also creates incentives for clinics to avoid serving patients with racial, ethnic, or socioeconomic complexities and needs."[185]

In effect, doctors are punished financially for caring for the most difficult patients. These value-based purchasing systems enable providers to make more money by putting relatively more energy into documenting care than providing it, essentially "gaming" the system.

The problem of "value-based" compensation systems exacerbating health disparities is not unique to Minnesota. A 2014 report commissioned by the Obama administration and convened by the National Quality Forum said that providers who serve low income people and communities, "are more likely to be identified as 'poor performers' and… more likely to face financial penalties in pay-for-performance programs." This can lead to "a series of adverse feedback loops that result in a 'downward spiral' of access and quality for those [socially and economically disadvantaged] populations. The net effect could *worsen* rather than ameliorate healthcare disparities."[186]

---

184 Minnesota Health Care Safety Net Coalition, "Recommendations on Health Disparities," September 11, 2015, p. 7, http://mn.gov/dhs/images/HCFTF-Disparities-Presentation-Handout-Safety-Net-9-11-15.pdf.
185 Ibid.
186 National Quality Forum, "Risk Adjustment for Socioeconomic

Even when those doctors and hospitals provide superior care, patients may have worse outcomes because of issues unrelated to their health: their inability to afford medications, difficulty in getting transportation to get care, and challenges in following medical instructions because of poor education or literacy problems.

While the *intent* of "report cards" on medical providers may be good, in practice the concept relies heavily on patient outcomes to indicate the quality of care given.

That practice is based on a faulty premise, no matter how accurate the testing and measurement. The vast majority of factors affecting patient outcomes are ones over which the doctor or clinic have no control. "Factors far outside the control of a doctor or hospital—patients' income, housing, education, even race—can significantly affect patient health, health care and providers' performance scores," Dr. Christine Cassel, President of the National Quality Forum, acknowledged.[187]

Properly adjusting for socioeconomic factors that impact outcomes would be incredibly difficult and expensive.

When the National Quality Forum attempted to address concerns raised by its panel about pay-for-performance increasing disparities, they offered some potential measures that some have suggested be used to adjust for socioeconomic factors that impact outcomes.

However, the report's comments on the difficulty of getting accurate measurements show the complexity of this endeavor. For example, data on patient income was

Status or Other Sociodemographic Factors," August 15, 2014, p. 16, http://www.qualityforum.org/Publications/2014/08/Risk_Adjustment_for_Socioeconomic_Status_or_Other_Sociodemographic_Factors.aspx.
187   Robert Pear, "Health Law's Pay Policy Is Skewed, Panel Finds," *New York Times*, April 27, 2014, http://www.nytimes.com/2014/04/28/us/politics/health-laws-pay-policy-is-skewed-panel-finds.html?_r=2.

described as "hard to collect" and its meaning "is not geographically consistent due to difference in costs of living."[188]

The report said that collecting information on literacy is challenging because there are "no standardized definitions" and it "may be easy to game." Measuring "social support" from family and neighbors available to the patient is difficult because it is a "multidimensional construct that typically requires multiple questions [to determine]" and there is a "lack of agreement about how to measure."[189]

Then, throw in numerous other factors—homelessness or housing instability, English proficiency, availability of transportation to the medical clinic, crime rate in the neighborhood, access to healthy foods—each of which may have an impact on patient outcomes more significant than the quality of medical care that this entire process is meant to measure, and you can see how expensive and inaccurate this process is.

"Quality" Payment Systems are Expensive and Counterproductive

Even if it were possible to *accurately* grade providers, there is no evidence that value-based purchasing would save money—certainly not enough to pay the enormous costs of conducting the measurements and administering the payment system.

Calling those administrative costs "enormous" is not an exaggeration. The title of a March 2016 study published in *Health Affairs*, summarized the scope of the costs:

---

188   National Quality Forum, "Risk Adjustment for Socioeconomic Status or Other Sociodemographic Factors," August 15, 2014, pp. 44-46, http://www.qualityforum.org/Publications/2014/08/Risk_Adjustment_for_Socioeconomic_Status_or_Other_Sociodemographic_Factors.aspx.
189   Ibid.

"US Physician Practices Spend More Than $15.4 Billion Annually to Report Quality Measures."[190] The report estimated that "the average physician spent 2.6 hours per week (enough time to care for approximately nine additional patients) dealing with quality measures; staff other than physicians spent 12.5 hours per physician per week dealing with quality measures." That's a total of over 15 hours required for every physician every week, just for the medical providers to report quality measures on which they are to be graded.[191]

On top of the harm caused by requiring medical professionals to fill out administrative paperwork instead of spending more time treating patients, and on top of financially penalizing providers who serve socially and economically disadvantaged people, value-based purchasing may *directly* affect care in an adverse manner, by interfering with medical judgment.

A medical doctor working in a Minneapolis clinic serving low income people explained[192] how the clinic director was encouraging the doctors to prescribe statins to patients with diabetes because it is one of the "quality" measures that affects the clinic's already-strained finances. The doctor was treating a patient with diabetes, but felt that prescribing a statin for that patient was questionable—a "50-50" call—because the patient had some complicating factors in addition to diabetes in which the statin might cause more harm. The doctor felt pressure to prescribe a statin in order to help the clinic look better on quality measures.

---

190 Lawrence P. Casalino, et al., "US Physician Practices Spend More Than $15.4 Billion Annually To Report Quality Measures," *Health Affairs* **35 (March 2016), pp. 3401-3406,** http://content.healthaffairs.org/content/35/3/401.abstract.
191 Ibid.
192 Personal communication, November 5, 2015.

This illustrates how application of "quality" measurements, tied to the finances of a low income clinic, can interfere with a medical doctor's best professional judgment. This is *not* the way to improve quality.

This does not mean that we shouldn't attempt to measure quality of care. It only means that we should not try to base provider compensation on "quality measurements." It is a flawed premise that we can determine the quality of providers based on patient outcomes, when there are so many factors outside of the provider's control. After huge investments of time and money, "Value-Based Purchasing" will likely increase health disparities by giving perverse incentives that punish some of the best providers, and discouraging them from giving care to those who most need it.

We must continuously work to improve care. But the goal of that quality improvement process should be to determine best practices and work with medical providers to implement those practices. Basing payments on inaccurate or misleading "quality measurements" is likely to reduce the quality of care, not increase it.

Managed Care is Actually Managed Insurance Losses

As mentioned above, supporters of various health reforms effectively discourage many people from questioning their proposals by using terminology that paints skeptics as anti-accountability, or unconcerned about value and quality.

For the last few decades, "capitated"[193] insurance plans have described themselves as "managed care

---

193 Capitation is a payment system based on a payment per person (per *capita*), often calculated per member, per month, where the health plan is paid to cover all care for the member of the health plan over a period of time rather than paying for the particular services and treatments provided to the member.

organizations," which gives the impression that they help manage a patient's care. However, this terminology does not reflect any real managing of the *patient's* care. In health care parlance, managed care is essentially the payment of funds to an insurance company to pay fee-for-service payments to providers, rather than having the payer provide those payments directly.

The only significant "managing" by the insurance plans is to reduce insurance company expenses by telling doctors and patients which services they will cover. While this managing may save money for the insurance company, it is not clear that it saves money for the patient or the employer paying the premiums, even if it is reducing the quality and timeliness of care.

Real *managed care* is something different than what we currently call managed care. Real managed care means having someone in a health clinic help patients manage their medical needs and navigate through the medical system.

C. Prior Reforms Were Based on Myths

Myth: "Fee-For-Service is the Problem"

Some people believe that payment reform means replacing the fee-for-service payment model with something different. As a result, Minnesota and other states have spent years experimenting with alternative forms of payment for medical providers. While we should always be looking for the most effective payment systems, it is important to recognize that there is no perfect means of compensation.

Several years ago, University of Minnesota health economist Jon Christianson jokingly said that while there are numerous means of paying medical providers, "the worst three are fee-for-service, capitation, and salary." He continued by pointing out that practically every form of provider payment is based on some combination of those three modes.[194]

Christianson suggested that we look at the incentives for each of those three options to see why each one is less than ideal. From a purely economic perspective, the incentive for **fee-for-service** is for the provider to "treat as *many* people for as *many* things as possible." The incentive for **capitation** is for the provider to "treat as *many* people for as *few* things as possible." The incentive for salary compensation of the provider is to "treat as *few* people for as *few* things as possible."[195]

Christianson used that intentionally cynical economic perspective to make his point that there is no means of compensating providers that does not have somewhat perverse incentives.

Fortunately, economics is only one factor motivating providers, and there are checks in the health care system that block those incentives from driving the way our health care system operates. The reality is that we currently pay providers, and will likely continue to pay them, through some combination of these payment modes.

Those who push for replacing fee-for-service (FFS) make two assumptions, which have been restated so many times that many health administrators and policy makers treat them as fact:

> Assumption #1: FFS causes overuse of our health care system, and

> Assumption #2: Overuse of our health care system is pervasive and the primary cause of our high costs.

---

194   Dr. Jon Christianson, "Paying Physicians: Comparing Single Payer Systems to the United States," Presentation at the University of Minnesota, Minneapolis, MN, May 9, 2008.
195   Ibid.

A concise summary of the fallacy of these two assumptions was presented and documented by Kip Sullivan and Ted Marmor in a 2015 issue of the *Yale Journal of Health Policy, Law, and Ethics*.[196]

"Neither assumption has ever been supported by research. At least four types of evidence contradict these assumptions:

- Evidence that citizens of many other industrialized nations consume medical services at or above American rates, and yet per capita spending on medical care in these countries is far below the American level;[197]

- research showing that underuse of medical care in the US is far more common than overuse, even among the insured;[198]

- evidence that research demonstrating overuse of specific medical services is virtually non-existent compared with the myriad goods and services delivered by clinics and hospitals and other providers in industrialized nations;[199]

---

196 Theodore R. Marmor and Kip Sullivan, "Medicare at 50: Why Medicare-for-all Did Not Take Place," *Yale Journal of Health Policy, Law, and Ethics* 15:1 (2015), p. 158-159, digitalcommons.law.yale.edu/yjhple/vol15/iss1/9/. There was a typo in the original, corrected in the quoted text here with permission from the authors. The following four citations come from the Marmor and Sullivan paper.
197 Marmor and Sullivan cite Gerard Anderson, et al., "It's the Prices, Stupid: Why the United States Is So Different From Other Countries," *Health Affairs* 22:3 (2003), p. 89, http://content.healthaffairs.org/content/22/3/89.full.pdf+html.
198 Marmor and Sullivan cite Elizabeth A. McGlynn, et al., "The Quality of Health Care Delivered to Adults in the United States," *New England Journal of Medicine* 348 (2003), p. 2635, http://www.nejm.org/doi/pdf/10.1056/NEJMsa022615.
199 Marmor and Sullivan include the following quotations in their citations (p. 158 n26): "The robust evidence about overuse in the US is limited to a few services." See Deborah Korenstein et al., "Overuse of Health Care Services in the United States: An Understudied Problem,"

- evidence that overuse occurs as often among providers paid FFS as among providers subject to the restrictions and incentives of managed care."[200]

Marmor and Sullivan continue,

> "Demonstrating the overuse of specific goods and services is complicated by the fact that uncertainty plays a role in many medical decisions. Many services, for example hospitalization and additional tests, are ordered to rule out a diagnosis or to otherwise reduce uncertainty. The fact that the patient turned out not to be so sick as to need hospitalization, or did not have the suspected disease, is not evidence of overuse.

> "Over the last decade, the evidence most often invoked by those who claim overuse is rampant are studies that show regional variation in the utilization rates of medical care. But this research does not tell us how much of the variation is due to overuse and how much to underuse."[201]

Archives of Internal Medicine 172:2 (2012), p. 171. "What is most striking about this report [i.e., Korenstein et al., previous quotation] is how hard the authors searched for data on overuse of health care and how little they found. They viewed 21 years of the medical literature and evaluated 114,831 publications, yet found only 172 articles that addressed overuse of health care." See Mitchell H. Katz, "Overuse of Health Care: Where Are the Data?" *Archives of Internal Medicine* 172:2 (2012), p. 178. "One factor that has often been cited as a probable cause of overuse is ... FFS payment.... In fact, a direct association between FFS payment and overuse has never been established. No study has used formal appropriateness criteria for specific procedures to compare rates of overuse in FFS financing versus other forms of payment." See Elise C. Becher & Mark R. Chassin, "Improving the Quality of Health Care: Who Will Lead?" *Health Affairs* 20 (2001), pp. 164, 166-67.

200   Marmor and Sullivan cite Salomeh Keyhani et al., "Overuse and Systems of Care: A Systematic Review," *Medical Care* 51:6 (2013), p. 503.

201   Marmor and Sullivan, p. 158 n26.

Rather than continue to push the American health care system further into the administrative complexity of ACOs, HMOs, VBP, P4P, and other payment reforms based on those false assumptions, it is time to save time and money by working to fix the real problems that make our health care system so costly and dysfunctional.

Lack of Evidence for Alternative Payment Models

When health policy makers propose or implement alternative payment models, those models are promoted as logical steps to reining in health care costs, despite the lack of evidence showing that these models would save money or improve care.

The assumption that fee-for-service causes high costs, and that the alternative models will fix it, is so prevalent that the proponents are seldom challenged for failing to produce supportive evidence.

Instead of studies showing their effectiveness, we are seeing growing evidence that the information that drove the push for ACOs and alternative payment models was not reliable.

We rightly talk about the need for "evidence-based *medicine*," but it is equally important that we use evidence-based *health policy*. As the health care system continues to rapidly implement and expand these alternative payment models, it is not sufficient to simply call for robust evaluation. Instead, we should stop all expansion of these bureaucratic, complex payment systems until proponents can show evidence that they will not make the system worse.

D. Real Payment Reform

In a multi-payer system, payment reform is difficult— financial interests of competing insurers get in the way. For example, health plans or "payers" will seldom begin reimbursing for services that their competitors don't cover, nor can they realistically lower the reimbursement rate for some services when others are paying more.

The simplicity of the Minnesota Health Plan makes such reform possible—there's only one plan to deal with. Under the MHP, the plan and providers would negotiate rates and a payment system. As a result, providers and the MHP could experiment with, modify, or adopt other payment modes, enabling them to negotiate better means of compensation.

Starting from Day 1, the MHP would implement several important payment reforms. In addition to savings from paying institutional providers with global budgets and from creation of a logical fee-for-service structure for other providers, the MHP would immediately implement the payment reform most needed: It would eliminate the insurance bureaucracy, where billions of dollars are wasted in the red tape of payment through multiple insurance companies, each of which covers different procedures and pays for them at different rates. This would all be replaced with a simple, fair reimbursement from the MHP that would pay all of the bills.

The Minnesota Health Plan doesn't just create opportunities for payment reform; it *is* payment reform.

8. Politics of Passing the MHP

The biggest obstacle to delivering health care to all Minnesotans is the politics of passing the legislation. Even some supporters of universal health care do not believe that it is politically feasible. As a result, public officials understandably seek out lesser proposals they think can pass.

Unfortunately, after several decades of passing well-intentioned "politically feasible" efforts to plug gaps in the existing system, we now have an even more complex and convoluted health care system that fails to cover many people, yet costs twice what most other nations pay for health care.[202]

When Barack Obama campaigned for President in 2008, he articulated a compelling vision of health care for everyone. He inspired people from all age groups, including many independents and Republicans. Unfortunately, after he became President he backed away from his rhetoric about health care as a right because he thought it would be too difficult to pass universal health care. Obama turned instead to an alternative that would cover more people, but his plan was not universal and did not provide comprehensive coverage, nor did it fundamentally fix the inherent problems in the system.

One commentator said "reading the (Affordable Care Act) bill would put most folks to sleep. We're talking hundreds of pages of mind-numbing details for policy wonks, lawyers, lobbyists and professional bureaucrats." The commentator described the ACA as largely "a piling on of what we already have: a dense thicket of health insurance

---

202 OECD, "Total Expenditure on Health Per capita," June 30, 2014, http://www.oecd-ilibrary.org/social-issues-migration-health/total-expenditure-on-health-per-capita_20758480-table2.

policies, most private but some government, with rules and regulations that few understand.... It's a system run by accountants, not by patients or doctors. It's not a free market and it's not socialism."[203]

In contrast to the thousands of pages of legislation required to create the ACA, the simplicity of the MHP requires legislation that takes only a few dozen pages and is readily understandable without requiring lawyers and accountants to interpret it.

In addition, by eliminating existing government health care programs and the complex insurance system we currently have, the Minnesota Health Plan would remove literally thousands of pages from Minnesota law books.

Both because of the Affordable Care Act's complexity and its failure to address the fundamental problems with our health care system, the ACA is much easier to attack than defend. A good argument can be made that it was one of the major causes of the loss of so many Democratic Congressional seats in 2010, the first election after its passage, and again in 2014, the first election after the troubled roll-out of the exchanges.

The attacks on President Obama were not any less harsh because he pushed the ACA—an insurance-based plan, modeled on a Republican proposal—instead of a universal health care plan. In fact, the Republican attacks frequently *call* the ACA "socialized medicine."

If the political attacks are just as harsh regardless of what plan is proposed, it would make sense to offer a plan that actually meets our needs—one that is simple, understandable, affordable, and accomplishes the goal of covering everyone.

---

203 Steven B. Young, "What's the Deal with Michele Bachmann and Sarah Palin?" *Legal Ledger Capitol Report*, April 16, 2010, http://politicsinminnesota.com/2010/04/young-what%E2%80%99s-the-deal-with-michele-bachmann-and-sarah-palin.

By doing so, when facing the inevitable political attacks, we have a plan that is defensible, one that meets the health care needs of every household, one that costs less,[204] and one that improves the health of Minnesotans. And, it is much easier for one to persuade others of the merits of a system if one is personally persuaded that the system has merit. It won't please ideologues, but most people are far more concerned about having affordable health care for their families than which politicians favor the plan.

Many Minnesota legislators and legislative candidates, including those from conservative rural districts, have publicly expressed support for the Minnesota Health Plan—they understand it and know that they can persuade their constituents of its merit.

In small towns and farm communities, where health insurance is most expensive, it is an easy political sell to support health care for all, instead of trying to explain a complex program which requires people to buy health insurance and creates a marketplace where they can buy insurance policies. Even now that the MNsure (health insurance) exchange is working better, success in shopping for a reasonable policy does not end concerns about whether one will be able to afford out-of-pocket costs, and it does nothing for families whose medical needs are dental problems, nor does it help those who need nursing home care.

A. Myths About the MHP

"Socialized Medicine" & Fear of Government Making Medical Decisions

In our highly polarized political climate, any proposal for health care reform pushed by Democrats will be attacked as "socialized medicine." Even the ACA, an insurance-based

---

204 See Chapter 5, "Economics of the MHP."

plan, largely modeled after former Massachusetts Republican Governor Mitt Romney's "Romneycare," which, in turn, was largely based on ideas from the conservative Heritage Foundation,[205] has been likened to "socialized medicine."[206]

Socialized medicine is a system where the government employs the health care providers and owns the facilities, such as in the U.S. Veterans' Administration or the British health care system.

The Minnesota Health Plan is not a system of socialized medicine—it relies primarily on private-sector providers. The MHP could be described as "Medicare Plus," where, similar to Medicare, health care is publicly financed (in the MHP, through progressive premiums) but delivered through existing doctors, clinics, and hospitals. Under the Minnesota Health Plan, doctors and hospitals that are in the private sector would remain in the private sector.

The biggest difference between the MHP and traditional Medicare is that, unlike Medicare, the MHP would not require co-payments and deductibles, and it would cover nursing home care, dental, and many other services not covered by Medicare.

Many of the people who express concerns about "socialized medicine" do so because they are worried that government will make medical decisions for them.

---

205 Avik Roy, "The Tortuous History of Conservatives and the Individual Mandate," *Forbes*, February 7, 2012, http://www.forbes.com/sites/theapothecary/2012/02/07/the-tortuous-conservative-history-of-the-individual-mandate, and Avik Roy, "How the Heritage Foundation, a Conservative Think Tank, Promoted the Individual Mandate," *Forbes*, October 20, 2011, http://www.forbes.com/sites/theapothecary/2011/10/20/how-a-conservative-think-tank-invented-the-individual-mandate.
206 James Beattie and Michael W Chapman, "Ben Carson Warns: 'Socialized Medicine Is Keystone to Establishment of a Socialist State,'" *CNS News*, October 11, 2013, http://cnsnews.com/news/article/james-beattie-and-michael-w-chapman/ben-carson-warns-socialized-medicine-keystone.

Under the Minnesota Health Plan, medical decisions are made by patients and their doctors, period. It is under our *current* system that medical decisions are often made by insurance companies or by government. And this intrusion in medical decision-making—from both insurance companies and government—has been getting worse in recent years.

That's why the entire debate about patient "choice" during the debate over the Affordable Care Act is ironic. Both President Obama's statement "if you like your health plan you can keep it," and the resulting uproar when some plans failed to qualify, miss the point. The question isn't a choice of *insurance plans*. People want their choice of doctors and other providers.

To see just how ridiculous the debate over "choice" of insurance plan is, recognize that Minnesota seniors have *over two dozen options* for prescription drug coverage under Medicare Part D.[207] Seniors don't want a choice of prescription drug *insurance* plans—the choice they want is the ability to access the drugs that they need when they need them and to be able to choose whether to pick them up at their local pharmacy or have them shipped through mail-order.

Their current "choice" of prescription drug plans occasionally leads to purchase of a plan where the insurer changes the drug formulary in the middle of the year, and the patient is required to continue paying the plan even though it no longer covers the medications they need.

Rationing

Related to the concern about who makes medical choices is the fear that, in order to save money, insurance

---

207 Q1Medicare.com, "2016 Stand-Alone Medicare Part D Prescription Drug Plans," https://q1medicare.com/PartD-SearchPDPMedicare-2016PlanFinder.php?state=MN.

companies and government agencies will ration care, affecting people's ability to get treatment.

Health care should **not** be rationed by either government or insurance companies. Under the MHP, decision making would be made in the context of the doctor/patient relationship. Neither insurance companies nor government would make decisions that should be made by patients and their medical providers.

The reality is that people, when their doctors and providers have a chance to discuss options with them, tend to be very good at "rationing" their own health care. Just because various tests and treatments are available doesn't make people want to go to the doctor and have more work done.

For example, when spine doctors and their patients discuss options thoroughly, many choose not to have costly surgery, selecting alternative treatments instead. For end-of-life care, if given an option through a living will (advance directive), most people choose less-intrusive care, such as choosing not to be resuscitated when they are terminally ill and in pain.

"Freedom of Choice" is limited under our current system, not the MHP. Not only does the MHP give people the ability to choose the medical providers they are comfortable with, it also gives people and their doctors the ability to make care decisions without "prior authorization" or other rationing by insurance companies or government.

Waiting Lines

Excessive waiting lines are an indication of inadequate capacity in the health care system. Sometimes people assume providing universal access to health care will mean wait times for those wanting or needing to see a health care provider.

The issue of "waiting lines" is often brought up in reference to Canada, which has a popular single health plan that covers everyone. It's true that Canada does have somewhat longer waiting lines than the U.S. for some non-urgent care. In 2013, 26% of patients in the US seeking a physician appointment waited six or more days, while in Canada this was true for 33% of patients.[208] For patients needing to see a specialist, 6% in the U.S. waited at least 2 months compared to 29% of patients in Canada.[209]

But some Canadian provinces are making progress,[210] and a Canadian organization tracking the issue points out that other countries with universal health care do well at addressing the issue: "as seen in many other countries with universal health systems, it is indeed possible to have timely access to medical care—long waits are not an unavoidable price to pay nor are they tolerated by their citizenry."[211]

As with our current system, there may be some waiting lines for those seeking certain non-urgent specialized care. As anyone who has sought an appointment with a dermatologist or certain other specialists knows, it can take months to get an appointment. However, those waiting lines would be reduced because the MHP has the tools to address provider shortages, and would be required to provide timely care.

---

208   Robin Osborn and Cathy Schoen, "2013 International Health Policy Survey in Eleven Countries," *The Commonwealth Fund*, November 2013, p. 11, http://www.commonwealthfund.org/~/media/Files/Publications/In the Literature/2013/Nov/PDF_Schoen_2013_IHP_survey_chartpack_final.pdf.
209   Ibid., p. 16.
210   "Since 2007, the WTA [Wait Time Alliance] has graded provincial wait-time performance... In the first five years, progress was made in most provinces to reduce wait times. For the past two years, the process has stalled and there have been setbacks in some provinces. However... improvements have taken place for most provinces in 2014." Wait Time Alliance, "Close the Gap: Report Card on Wait Times in Canada," June 2014, p. 4, http://www.waittimealliance.ca/wp-content/uploads/2014/06/FINAL-EN-WTA-Report-Card.pdf.
211   Ibid., p. 2.

B. Making the Minnesota Health Plan a Reality

Powerful Financial Interests Strongly Oppose the MHP

Although the MHP would provide huge benefits, both financially and in terms of health and wellness, it may be the most difficult political battle of our age.

President Harry Truman began pushing for universal health care back in the 1940s and there have been a number of efforts to implement it over the last seventy years, but none has yet been successful.[212]

The difficulty of enacting this legislation comes from powerful financial interests defending the current system.

For example, during the six years prior to passage of the Affordable Care Act, Senator Max Baucus, received $3.8 million in contributions from insurance and health industry donors.[213]

Baucus, Chair of the Senate Finance Committee which ultimately drafted the 2010 health care legislation, refused to even hear testimony from doctors and nurses who were pleading for universal health care.

When asked why he would not consider universal health care when holding hearings on health care reform, Baucus said, "Well, just to be honest, it's not on the table—

---

212 "Truman was strongly committed to a single universal comprehensive health insurance plan. Whereas FDR's 1938 program had a separate proposal for medical care of the needy, it was Truman who proposed a single egalitarian system that included all classes of society, not just the working class." See Karen S. Palmer, MPH, MS, "A Brief History: Universal Health Care Efforts in the US," talk given at the Spring 1999 meeting of Physicians for a National Health Plan (PNHP) in San Francisco. Transcript available at http://www.pnhp.org/facts/a-brief-history-universal-health-care-efforts-in-the-us.
213 Open Secrets: Center for Responsive Politics, "Sen. Max Baucus: Top 20 Industries Contributing to Campaign Cmte and Leadership PAC, 2005-2010," http://www.opensecrets.org/politicians/industries.php?type=C&cid=N00004643&newMem=N&cycle=2010. Note contributions from the following industries: insurance, health professionals, pharmaceuticals/health products, health services/HMOs, and hospitals/nursing homes.

the only thing that's not—because it cannot pass. It just cannot pass."[214]

After passage of the ACA, Baucus "singled out" Liz Fowler, his chief health advisor, as the person who put together his health team and who wrote the document that "became the basis, the foundation, the blueprint from which almost all health care measures in all bills on both sides of the aisle came."[215]

The woman Baucus chose to lay out the blueprint for the ACA was a former vice president for WellPoint, one of the nation's largest health insurance companies.[216]

It is not surprising that the end result of the ACA legislation reflected goals of those powerful financial interests more than the goal of affordable, universal health care.

We cannot allow the insurance industry and the pharmaceutical lobby to continue to win. The tide may turn as the situation is becoming more urgent, as the current system is bankrupting the economy. Back in 1960, health expenditures in the United States were only 5% of the Gross Domestic Product (GDP). By 2014, those health expenditures had more than tripled as a portion of our economy, up to 17.5% of GDP.[217] We must win this fight.

---

214 Julie Rovner, NPR interview with Senator Max Baucus. Transcript available on *Bill Moyers' Journal*, May 22, 2009, http://www.pbs.org/moyers/journal/05222009/transcript4.html
215 Jane Hamsher, "Baucus Thanks Wellpoint VP Liz Fowler for Writing Health Care Bill," *ShadowProof*, March 29, 2010, http://fdlaction.firedoglake.com/2010/03/29/baucus-thanks-wellpoint-vp-liz-fowler-for-writing-health-care-bill.
216 Tom Curry, "Fact or Fiction? Senate Chairman Has Ties to Big Insurer," *MSNBC*, October 2, 2009, http://www.nbcnews.com/id/33129315/#.V7y9H-ZteUp.
217 See "NHE Summary including share of GDP, CY 1960-2014" available at Centers for Medicare and Medicaid Services (CMS), "National Health Expenditure Data: Historical," https://www.cms.gov/research-statistics-data-and-systems/statistics-trends-and-reports/nationalhealthexpenddata/nationalhealthaccountshistorical.html.

Polls Show Support for Universal Care and *Strong* Support for MHP Principles

While there are powerful financial interests who oppose it, the public is supportive of a universal health care system. A February 2016 Kaiser Family Foundation national poll asked: "Do you favor or oppose having guaranteed health insurance coverage in which all Americans would get their insurance through a single government health plan?" They found 50% of people support it while 43% oppose it.[218] Although the Minnesota Health Plan would deliver health care through the current, largely private, mix of health providers, this poll likely reflects what people think the system would entail.

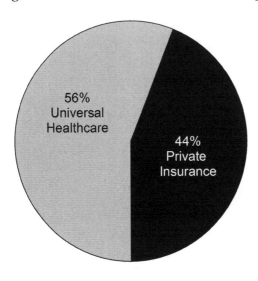

Minnesota polls also show wide public support for a universal system. In 2004, during Republican Governor Tim Pawlenty's Administration, the Governor's Council on Developmental Disabilities and the Minnesota Board on Aging conducted a poll which found: 56% prefer a "universal system where the government insures that everyone has health coverage" vs. 44% who prefer a "private system that relies on individuals and employers

---

218 Kaiser Family Foundation, "Kaiser Health Tracking Poll: February 2016," p. 5, http://files.kff.org/attachment/topline-methodology-kaiser-health-tracking-poll-february-2016.

to provide for their own health care needs."[219]

That same poll showed the public strongly supports some of the principles behind the MHP. An overwhelming 94% believe: "I should be able to choose any health care provider I want, including physicians and hospitals." 92% believe: "People should not be turned away from necessary medical treatment, even if they are uninsured and cannot afford the treatment."[220] By more than a 15 to 1 margin, Minnesotans support principles like these.

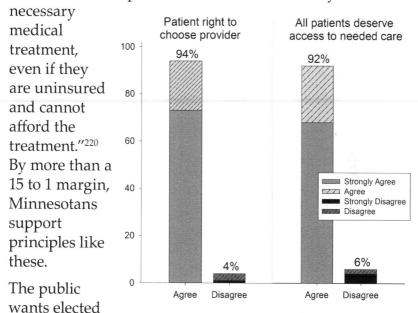

The public wants elected officials to fix the health care system and make sure that everyone has access to the care they need. Minnesota physicians also consider a "single-payer financing system" to be the best way to finance care, with 64% in favor of a single-payer system, according to a scientific survey published by Minnesota Medicine in 2007.[221]

219 Minnesota Health Care Poll, by the Governor's Council on Developmental Disabilities and the Minnesota Board on Aging, January 9, 2004, p. 20, https://mn.gov/mnddc/extra/customer-research/mn-health-care-opinion.pdf.
220 Ibid., p. 28.
221 Joel M. Albers, et al., "Single-Payer, Health Savings Accounts, or Managed Care? Minnesota Physicians' Perspectives," *Minnesota Medicine* 90 (February 2007).

9. How the Transition Would Occur

Moving from the world's most fragmented, administratively complex, and expensive health care system to one that is simple, understandable, and administratively efficient will not be easy, but Minnesotans can make it happen.

Keep in mind that our current system is too complicated and too disruptive—not just for a one-time event like this transition, but week after week, year after year. In fact, most of the challenge of implementing this transition would be due to the difficulty of creating an orderly process for closing out our complex, bureaucratic system.

The simplicity of the new health care system is beneficial immediately—the comparison between the costly, troubled roll-out of the health insurance exchanges like MNsure, versus the quick, simple enrollment of virtually all American seniors in Medicare back in 1966 illustrates that point.

Federal Waivers

There are a number of federal laws and rules from which Minnesota would need waivers in order to fully implement the Minnesota Health Plan. Obtaining the necessary approval either through federal administrative waivers or federal law will require significant effort. But to keep this in perspective, it will be a far bigger challenge to *pass* the MHP into law than to get federal approval.

The "innovation" waiver available beginning in January 2017, under Section 1332 of the Affordable Care Act (ACA), is designed to assist states in implementing alternatives to the ACA. While section 1332 does not cover all federal laws and rules from which the MHP would need exemptions, it directs federal agencies to work collaboratively with states and allow a single application to cover several of the waivers.

Minnesota will have a strong case with the federal government. In passing the MHP, Minnesota would be the only state to provide *comprehensive* health coverage to *all* of its residents, the only state to remove the administrative hassle from businesses and families of "shopping" for health insurance, and the only state to design an efficient, high quality health system that both saves money and addresses care delivery problems such as shortages of providers.

In the event that the state is unable to secure any of the waivers, the MHP Board is directed to work around those limitations, in a manner that best fulfills the principles of the MHP.[222]

A. An Outline of the Transition

Without minimizing the difficulty of this transition, here is a look at some basic steps involved in implementing a transition of this significance.

1. Pass the Minnesota Health Plan bill through the legislature for the governor's signature.

2. The Commissioner of Health would determine health plan regions, with county boards beginning the process of selecting regional health plan boards, and subsequent appointment of the Minnesota Health Plan Board.

3. The MHP Board would begin hiring staff and designing the structure of the system and working with state agencies on waiver approvals.

4. The Commissioners of Human Services, Health, and Minnesota Management & Budget (MMB) would work with the federal administration and Minnesota's congressional delegation to prepare

---

222 tinyurl.com/MHP-2016-bill, p. 9.24.

and make a request for necessary waivers from federal law and rule.

5. Upon receiving approvals of necessary waivers (and/or MHP action to design work-around alternatives if the state is unable to secure some or all desired waivers) the Board would:

a. create a timeline for implementation of the transition;

b. hire staff;

c. establish a budget;

d. develop proposed premiums and other revenue sources; and

e. implement extensive education and outreach to providers, the public, and businesses about the Minnesota Health Plan.

6. The MHP would work with the legislature if any accommodations are needed related to federal waivers and establish and prepare for assessment of individual premiums and business payroll taxes.

7. The MHP and providers would negotiate initial payment rates and reimbursement policies and procedures.

8. The MHP would select a claims processing firm (likely one of the existing health plans that has a claims processing system in place)

9. The MHP would work with employees and employers in the health insurance industry to plan for dislocated worker programs and services.

10. The MHP would create a plan for enrollment, including simple online and in person options. Those who are not pre-enrolled could be signed

up quickly at their first visit to a medical provider after the plan takes effect.

11. Transition Day. For Minnesotans, the change would be easier than the one they go through when they transition to Medicare on their 65th birthday, but there would be similarities:

>   **a. Little change in how health care is accessed.** Minnesotans continue going to their medical providers and setting up future appointments with their doctors, dentists, optometrists, physical therapists, and clinics, as needed.

>   **b. Big change in how health care is funded.** Minnesota families stop paying deductibles, co-pays, co-insurance, and premiums to other health plans, and begin paying premiums to the MHP. The MHP begins paying providers.

After initial implementation of the MHP, the plan, along with providers and businesses, would continue working on further improvements in public health, health care access, quality of care, and administrative efficiencies.

Every step of this transition to the Minnesota Health Plan would be challenging, but the current system's economic, administrative, and political challenges are even greater. And, unlike our current system, the MHP would successfully address the most important challenge of all: giving all Minnesotans access to comprehensive health care when they need it.

B. Closing Down the Insurance Exchange

Minnesota spent $189 million in federal grants to establish MNsure,[223] the state insurance exchange, only

---

223 Office of the Legislative Auditor, "Evaluation Report: Minnesota Health Insurance Exchange (MNsure)," February 2015, p. 19, http://www.

a few years ago. Under our current health care system, where some people need to purchase individual health insurance policies, it was logical to establish what is essentially an online "shopping center" for insurance plans.

Since the Minnesota Health Plan would replace health insurance with health care, there would no longer be any need for people to shop for health insurance.[224] Consequently, there would no longer be a need for MNsure.

At first glance, this may seem unfortunate because of that large initial investment. However, since the efficiency of the MHP avoids all of the hassle and expense that people experience from enrolling and re-enrolling on an annual basis, it is a significant benefit to Minnesota to be able to close the exchange. Plus, this creates an additional permanent, on-going savings: Minnesotans would save $44 million per year by eliminating the operating costs for MNsure.[225]

auditor.leg.state.mn.us/ped/pedrep/mnsure.pdf.

224   tinyurl.com/MHP-2016-bill, p. 25.24.

225   Office of the Legislative Auditor, "Evaluation Report: Minnesota Health Insurance Exchange (MNsure)," February 2015, p. 20, http://www.auditor.leg.state.mn.us/ped/pedrep/mnsure.pdf.

Epilogue: It's Time for the Minnesota Health Plan

Our current system, even with MNsure and the Affordable Care Act, still leaves many people without health coverage. Equally troubling, many Minnesotans who have health coverage still cannot afford the care they need.

Health *insurance* coverage fails to guarantee that people have access to health care, because insurance frequently excludes coverage for needed care such as dental, chemical dependency treatment, mental health, or long-term care.

Health insurance also requires significant out-of-pocket expenses, and it buries people and businesses with a thicket of confusing medical insurance applications and paperwork.

Despite our excellent medical providers and medical technology, Minnesota's system is so dysfunctional that many families cannot access it even when they have insurance.

It's time to stand up to the strong, well-financed opposition from the insurance industry and the pharmaceutical lobby.

We must replace health *insurance* for some with health *care* for all.

When European nations, Canada, and Japan are able to deliver comprehensive health care to all of their people, with better health outcomes, for roughly half the cost per person that we are currently spending, it is not an insurmountable challenge.

The Minnesota Health Plan would be an efficient health care system based on, and governed by, principles that ensure that all people receive high quality health care.

Minnesota has some of the best medical education, training, research, and technology in the world. It's time we adopt a health care system to match.

About the Author

Early in life, John Marty was taught to respect the dignity of all people and the importance of caring for others.

John's father, author and theologian Martin Marty, and his mother Elsa, were advocates for social justice and active in the civil rights movement. They taught him values which became deeply rooted in him.

After winning an upset victory to the Minnesota Senate in 1986, John quickly became known statewide for his work in government ethics and campaign finance reform.

Often far ahead of the political process, John consistently works for the well-being of all, even when those efforts are, initially, highly unpopular—such as his leadership on LGBT equality, since the beginning of his public service thirty years ago.

Beginning in 1987, Senator Marty introduced and passed the nation's first ban on smoking in hospitals and health care facilities. Long before such efforts gained public and political support, John worked for bans on mercury in consumer products, creation of a legal structure for public benefit corporations, for policies to create a fair economy with living wage jobs, early childhood education, domestic violence prevention, and numerous other critical issues.

Senator Marty was integral to the passage of legislation to speed up the transition of Minnesota's economy from fossil fuels to renewable energy, including Minnesota's community solar program.

Since his first years in office, John authored legislation to reduce the special interest money in politics. He passed a law prohibiting lobbyists and interest groups from giving gifts to public officials and sharply limiting the size of campaign contributions. John walks the talk, and personally rejects all special interest money, accepting No PAC money. No lobbyist money. No soft money. No large contributions, period.

John's ideas, including the Minnesota Health Plan proposed in this book, are based on principles rather than popularity. Through persistent prodding and advocacy, many of his ideas gain acceptance and become law in Minnesota. Many have been adopted in other states as well.

Senator Marty has co-chaired the Legislative Commission on Ending Poverty and the Legislative Energy Commission. He currently chairs the Senate Environment and Energy Committee, and is the former chair of the Health and Housing Committee.

John has received numerous awards for his leadership in government reform, environmental protection, disability rights, mental health, and economic and social justice.

A collection of John's columns on public policy are available at www.apple-pie.org.

Senator Marty is a graduate of St. Olaf College with a degree in Ethics and Society. He is in his ninth term in the Minnesota Senate. John lives in Roseville with his wife Connie.